BURN
IT
DOWN

SEVEN DAYS
TO
REFORGE YOUR LIFE

JAMES SHERIDAN

Burn It Down © 2025 Dodd Mead & Co.ᴛᴍ

Paperback ISBN: 979-8-9939128-0-6
Hardcover ISBN: 979-8-9939128-1-3
eBook ISBN: 979-8-9939128-2-0

Library of Congress Control Number - 2026900013

Published by Dodd Mead & Co. ᴛᴍ
Newport Beach, California

Disclaimer: This book is a work of personal and psychological exploration.
It is not a substitute for professional mental health care, medical treatment,
or therapy. Nothing in these pages is intended to diagnose, treat, or cure any
condition. If you are experiencing acute distress, self-harm thoughts, or a mental
health crisis, please seek qualified professional support. Use the ideas and
practices in this book at your own pace and with your own discernment.

www.DoddMead.Co

CONTENTS

To optimize your experience,
activate your complimentary
7-day digital workbook.

Go to www.BurnItDown.online/begin
or scan below:

*"And so long as you haven't experienced this:
to die and so to grow, you are only
a troubled guest on the dark earth."*
— Goethe

DAY **1**

GROUND ZERO

Fired up

Our darkest hour is the staging post of our finest hour.

Perhaps you lost all your money, lost a job, lost a home, lost a love, lost mobility or all of those things. Perhaps you never had anything worth losing. Perhaps it's you who is lost.

But you're still breathing.

And if you're still breathing, you can *and will* walk out of the fire, reborn and unstoppable.

Fire destroys. But it also lights the darkness and facilitates renewal.

It reforges.

If your life is in pieces, we aren't here to glue those pieces back together. If it broke, it was weak in the first place.

And if your life isn't in pieces (yet)?

We're going to break it into pieces, anyway. And reforge it.

Into something unbreakable.

You have a rendezvous with destiny, like it or not. And *not* liking it is perhaps why the fire started in the first place.

I don't speak from the high ground. Like so many of us, I had to learn all this the hard way...

My life had crashed and burned. Personal, professional, you name it. Rock-bottom.

It was as if I'd been playing on train tracks for years but only suddenly noticing the oncoming train before it splattered me.

Maybe deep down I wanted to splatter.

My second ex-wife, Jenna, found me passed out in her spare bedroom, an almost empty vodka bottle in one hand, and a Glock 20 pistol in the other. I vaguely recall hearing her say, "What the fuck?" when she first saw me there. Then I heard her scream, "What the fuck!?" when she saw what I was holding. I was half asleep as she gently pulled the gun from my cold fingers and darted out of the room with it.

I later woke up, my head aching as my face sank from the realization that my life wasn't just a bad dream, after all.

While I had slept, Jenna had called my mother back in England and they had arranged for me to fly "home" for seven days.

Their plan made sense. England. A place where you'd probably go to jail for even thinking about guns. But I'd been living in Florida for years, so maybe I was out of touch.

I thought it was a ridiculous idea. I swept it aside and continued the pity-party, living in my ex-wife's spare bedroom, drowning sorrows in cheap vodka.

Every day was a replay. Yesterday bled into tomorrow; there was never a today. It was as if I lived in a glass sphere, watching normal people move through happy lives on the outside.

Around a week later, I woke up in the middle of the night because of what seemed like a runny nose. I walked into the bathroom and saw blood streaming down my face. It was a heavy nosebleed, cause unknown.

I sobbed over the bloodied sink.

Blood and tears.

Sweat was the only thing missing.

A few days later, I felt tingles in my left arm and my chest felt like a washing machine full of golf balls. "Oh, God. No. Oh, God."

I was no doctor, but I thought I knew what this meant. The blood drained from my face. I was suddenly terrified that I might lose... *lose what?* The life that evidently wasn't worth a damn, anyway?

They rushed me to the hospital. When a middle-aged guy complaining about chest pains and a loss of sensation on one side walks into the ER, they don't screw around. Within ten minutes, I was admitted and connected to every monitor they could find.

I wondered if they'd even find a pulse, but I let myself be swept along and swallowed up, encircled by caregivers.

A parade of nurses and doctors came and went.

After two days of tests, I was oddly sad to admit the chest pain and left-side tingles had subsided. In fact, the doctors scratched their heads after the ultrasound and treadmill as they playfully declared, "Dude, there's nothing wrong with you. You're actually in great shape!"

According to medicine, anyway.

Is there a blood test that shows when a person has lost their soul? Is there a DNA test that tells us what the point of it all is? Does an ultrasound of the heart reveal when it's been broken one time too many?

Right before they discharged me, Jenna sat at my bedside while my mother called to ask me to "come home for seven days."

"Why?" I said, sucking on a juice box I couldn't taste, "I don't see the point."

Jenna frowned, eyes steady on me. "Because you need this."

She'd always said I had a self-destruct button that I kept on pushing.

"Right now," I replied, "I need a depressing English winter like I need a bullet to the brain." Considering recent events, I realized the phrase to be a little too true for comfort, but it was out of my mouth now.

An awkward pause.

"I got the ticket," my mother said.

One thing about growing up on the flight path of London Heathrow airport and being raised by an airline family is that there was never a shortage of plane tickets to throw around. I thought it was a pointless idea, but I went along.

As I was packing, burrowing through what was left of my belongings in a tiny closet, my eye caught a leather document pouch that had been buried under a pile of junk.

I stared at it and gulped. It filled me with shame.

Why?

Okay. Do you want to know the *really* insane part about all this? The really embarrassing part. The part that made me want to "fall on my sword," to borrow a shamed samurai's poetic end...

I had made my fortune as a "guru." A personal development, wealth-building, health-building, motivational "guru."

For decades I had been telling people how *not* to do exactly what I had done, to avoid the mistakes I had made, to "never give up" the way I was giving up.

Vodka. I was the one people came to for answers. Years of guiding others, standing on stages, speaking truths that *felt* solid. Until one day, I found myself in the very abyss I thought I had taught others to climb out of. The kind of collapse that makes a mockery of everything you once believed. The kind that doesn't ask questions— it just takes.

And now that I was the one who needed help, when it came to swallowing my own medicine I had spat it out.

That leather document pouch I saw in the closet contained all my personal development teaching notes. It even contained the tiny microphone I'd tape to my face at seminars; now it seemed like a museum piece. An artifact of shame.

I hadn't read these notes for years. I didn't open the leather pouch, but I felt strangely compelled to pack it. I dropped it into my carry-on bag as if it was a soiled diaper.

As I boarded the British Airways plane on a stormy night in Miami, I glared at the economy seat I'd been allocated. It seemed absurdly small. On a night flight, I was expected to sleep in this crib of a seat. I used to fly business class so often I took it for granted. Was this my new life?

I listened to the captain do his briefing and wondered why the hell I hadn't remained an airline captain (my former life), cruising through an easy career, and soon to be retired.

I felt ashamed to the bone, as if the other passengers now filling the cabin were laughing at me with my tiny seat. I grumbled a coping strategy to myself, hoping the whole cabin would somehow hear me: "I'll just bury myself in martinis, movies, and melatonin until I pass the fuck out, then this nightmare will be over."

I settled into my crib. The first movie I pulled up on my iPad was *Fight Club*, and half an hour in, Brad Pitt tried to console me. He said, "You know, man, it could be worse. A woman could cut off your penis while you're sleeping and toss it out the window of a moving car."

There's always that.

Only I didn't even have a woman to cut off my penis, said one voice in my head—for the first time in my adult life, I wasn't in a serious relationship. Another voice said: Brad's right. It could be worse.

My eyes wandered down to my carry-on backpack jammed under my feet, and the leather document pouch shoved inside it. That *Fight Club* scene reminded me of a story from an ancient text (*The*

Dhammapada) I knew was somewhere in the thick stack of notes in that pouch:

Buddha visited a village that was suffering from a plague. A woman ran out to him, distraught over her son recently dying.

"Oh, Buddha! Please help me. I am lost in sorrow. Is there anything you can do?"

Buddha said, "Yes. Bring me some mustard seed from someone else's house."

The woman dutifully agreed.

As she was walking away, Buddha added, "But this mustard seed must come from a household that has not experienced death."

The woman agreed.

Hours passed, and Buddha waited.

Eventually, the woman returned, exasperated. "Buddha, I cannot find such a household."

And the lesson was learned.

Bah. Self-help playbook, I thought.

I had helped so many people by speaking this way, but did I believe in it myself? Did I feel it? *Did I live it?*

Perhaps this was a start.

I abandoned the "martinis, movies, melatonin, and pass the fuck out" plan. I plucked out the leather document pouch and started reading like a stern critic.

As I read into the night, bumping through trans-Atlantic turbulence, surrounded by snoring passengers, the tiny spotlight above seemed like an interrogation lamp.

Two realizations slapped me in the face:

I hadn't practiced a lot of what I'd preached.

And who cares because I didn't agree with a lot of this material anymore, anyway!

But there was a silver-lining. The steady accumulation of all these notes reminded me of those past years. How I had stared down the barrel of a gun several times before, in different ways, under different skies.

And I had prevailed.

I used to laugh in the face of adversity, burning naysayers as my rocket fuel. Whenever someone would tell me "It can't be done" or "that's impossible," I would actually get excited.

What had changed?

Why was I struggling to relight the "rocket engines" one last time?

The plane slumped onto a damp runway on a March morning that was even gloomier than I'd expected in London. I couldn't bear to see my reflection as the automated customs gate took my picture before letting me pass. Catatonic, I sank down an escalator and snaked through a blur of underground passageways to baggage reclaim. Then I met my mother on the other side.

I knew I was now a mere shade of the vibrant and successful son who once had it all, and I felt ashamed to stand there before her. Not that she would ever judge me because of it. We hugged. I wanted to cry but I knew it would upset her and only add to my shame.

After sleepwalking to her car, I slept all the way to her house, drifting in and out of sleep, as we drove west into afternoon sun. A strange dream. I felt like a half-dead soldier who'd just been airlifted from the battlefield.

When we arrived in Somerset, she showed me the tiny spare room she'd prepared for me. My "life story" photo album lay on a lovingly made collapsible bed. The room had navy walls and a small circular window speckled with rain. My cave for the week.

When she left the room, I placed the half-empty photo album on my lap but didn't open it. I just stared at the jacket.

The contents of that photo album now seemed to have been for nothing; a record of decades of "success," work, relationships, and striving. And all the fruits of it, now smoke and ash.

And that's when I wondered (again) if there was any point to going on.

Could I really pull myself back up and do it all over again?

Did I even want to? Was it worth it? The struggle, the trials, the effort.

The shame and embarrassment, even if I tried.

How could I speak from a position of authority after what had happened to me? Not being a hypocrite was perhaps the last virtue I had left.

Afternoon sun caught the tiny window and lit my cave.

Then I stared at the photo album jacket again. I contemplated what lay inside it.

Is that how the half-empty album should end? With failure. My final self-help "lesson" to my children and all who looked up to me: "When life knocks you on your ass... head for the exit."

Since disaster had crept up on me, life had felt surreal—like I'd walked into an episode of *The Twilight Zone.*

A familiar smell from the kitchen sparked childhood memories.

And then, in that feeling, recalling *The Twilight Zone*— that old TV show I watched with my mother as a child— I remembered something about it: there was usually a moral to the story in those supernatural thrillers...

The character in each episode was often getting a trial by fire, *a role-reversal,* a warning, or a second chance in a "ghosts of Christmas past" kind of way.

I imagined how my episode might look had my story been on the show:

Me crying in a corner on the floor, half-naked, surrounded by ashes, as a dark and smoldering demon towered over me, growling, "For years you've been giving all this advice to others... not from a position of experience but from your ivory tower! Ha. Well, now you're in the shoes of those who came to you for help; broken, ruined, desperate, and directionless... Now let's see *you* dig your way out..."

The frivolous distraction jarred my mind and a shudder went down my spine. That demon's voice was too real. It felt more like an intervention than an imagining. And I felt something shift within.

For months I had been asking, "Why did this happen to *ME?!*"

Suddenly, I found myself asking, "*WHY* did this happen to me?"

Same sentence, different emphasis on a single word... it changes everything.

Everything.

Say the same thing differently and witness a death sentence transform into a mission statement...

Witness a self-pitying victim transform into an empowered human being about to embark on the ultimate journey...

Witness a glimpse of a future promise enter the void...

Simply witness.

Why did this happen?

I'm not talking about the superficial and obvious: "because a car hit me," "because my partner left me," "because I lost my job," "because they died of cancer." We're looking for the deeper reason.

What if the worst thing that happened to you was the only thing that could have shaped you into what you were meant to become?

That was the moment I saw it differently. Not as a curse, but as raw material.

Our life is now on a different trajectory. Like a meteor bumped off course by a collision with another meteor, now headed for a different galaxy, a new timeline.

A reset.

We may not like it, but there is no denying it.

Sometimes disaster strikes as a way of forcing us onto the true path. And I know it sucks to hear that right now, but what are the alternative ways of looking at it? That events are completely random and there is no point to it all? That God hates us? That one should seek vengeance?

Where are those viewpoints taking us?

Nowhere good.

The skeptic might argue, "Bullshit. We choose our own destiny."

I think that's a common confusion that needs clearing up:

We choose our own *future*.

But destiny is not the future; it's one of many *possible* futures. Destiny just happens to be one possible future we can choose to live. A future that, for reasons we'll explore later, is the optimal path for us through life— a path that, *if we are paying attention to the serendipitous clues*, will reveal itself to us—we'll return to this idea on Day 7.

Whether we choose to follow that path or not is up to us because we choose our future. But crisis will keep nudging or slapping us until we pay attention to it.

We choose our future, not our destiny.

From a certain point of view— the *constructive* point of view— there appears to be a hidden meaning behind all events, and it is serving our evolution. The deeper reason may not yet be clear, but before the end of this book I will make it clear.

All I ask from you now is that you simply be *open* to the idea that there *is* a reason for where you are right now. However unjust. However cruel. However heart wrenching. However twisted.

Have faith in the WHY.

I know that's a hard idea to swallow, so allow me to build on it.

Things have not gone according to plan. Maybe that's an understatement. But nevertheless, the pain we feel now is because what we expected to happen in our lives did not happen, right?

In other words, pain, struggle, disappointment, and sadness are all a function of life *not meeting our expectations.*

So, what if our expectations were flawed?

What if we got the expected 'dream delivery date' wrong? You know that invisible date or age we set for ourselves—the one by which we thought we'd have "made it."

Prophecy over punishment

There are no broken dreams if the dream isn't over.

Things have happened. Things have not happened. We have regrets. We've fantasized about owning a time machine that could whisk us back to those critical plot points in our life— a story that we've rewritten a thousand times in our heads, starting with these two words:

"If *only*..."

If *only* we'd made a different choice back then, our life would look a lot different today.

Yes, life could well have looked a lot different today; possibly a lot *worse*.

The thing is, we don't know for sure that the things that did or didn't happen are "good" or "bad" *because our life story remains unfinished.* And it will never be fully told if we don't move our story forward.

We need to zoom out from this moment in our lives and see the bigger picture.

Our personal history is a one-sided story, a *one-way* road taken at the expense of other roads that each led to unknowns that *shall remain unknowns.*

We know *nothing* about how our lives would have panned out had things happened or not happened to us, *because our life story remains unfinished.*

We don't know the ending yet.

When the 19th century philosopher, Schopenhauer, looked back on his life, he said it often appeared to have a certain structure, with events seeming to be interconnected, like the plot points of a story. Like things were meant to happen, contributing to a bigger and meaningful picture. He conceded that this could've been purely our minds creating such a structure to try to make sense of it all, rather than some kind of divine intervention or providence.

Jung offered an explanation that straddled both sides of Schopenhauer's argument with what he called "synchronicity;" the idea of meaningful coincidences.

Whether there *is* a hidden structure to it all or we are unconsciously *creating* such a structure to make sense of it, it's all the same:

There is a structure to our individual life stories.

That's why all good stories have structure. A structure that helps us find meaning, just as a young child tries to make sense of the world they are suddenly born into.

A cherished theme of Hinduism is that Krishna (God) created the world as his play, and we are the characters who perform a story upon it, each with different roles to play. Ancient Greeks articulated the concept of tragedy into theater, to remind us of the things that happen and that it is all part of nature.

What ancient Greeks and Hindus were trying to say is, "Life is like this." Art is life, or it wouldn't be art. Art is not art unless it resonates with our souls.

Today, Hollywood is our theater, and the same message is subliminally woven into the movies that move us, particularly in terms of this hidden structure behind the action and dialogue.

"Life isn't a movie," some might say. When it comes to this hidden structure, I disagree.

Good movies aren't an escape from life; they're a guidebook *about* life. As movie critic, Kenneth Burke said, "Stories are equipment for living." The screenplay schoolmaster, Robert McKee said, "Story isn't a flight from reality but a vehicle that carries us on our search for reality."

And the quintessential story is one where there is a "death" and a "resurrection."

There can be no resurrection without death. Not the kind of death where our heart stops. I mean the kind of death where our heart *starts*. Where it stops being shoved into second place behind our mind.

This storyline of death and rebirth is evidently written into our genes as much as into our most ancient and cherished texts. It's metaphor language for a fall from grace and a comeback. This is why underdog and Cinderella plots are so powerful and moving for us, because deep down we know that "Life is like this."

Or, at least, life could... and should be like this.

Whether it actually does play out like that or not is in *our hands*.

The best stories are ones of transformation, and they follow a classic story structure:

We see the protagonist's life irreversibly altered by an event.

There is *change*.

Then there is a long *struggle* as the protagonist tries to dig a way out of the crisis.

And along the way, there is a *change* to their character. The journey— *the change and the struggle*— is making them stronger and more complete. They find their true nature and transform into a more complete individual.

The message? There was at least one section in my self-help playbook pouch that I still agreed with— *had* to agree with— even if I was yet to walk this talk:

Yes, there is a mountain to climb. But the climbing of it is what makes us. And sometimes we finally get what we want only to discover that now we don't want it, because of who we became on the journey.

Superhero stories usually start with a personal catastrophe that ends up being for the better only when they embraced the catastrophe. When they *surrendered* to destiny.

And would any movie ending be as meaningful *without* struggle? Screenwriters know that only conflict and adversity can drive a story forward. And this resonates with us because "life is like this."

So, with a big picture view, what if nothing is going wrong in our story?

Stories, like life, have a three-act structure. It plays out something like this (note the emphasis):

Act One: Throw hero into dark pit.

Act Two (the longest act by far): Throw rocks at hero in dark pit. *At very end of Act Two, push hero to breaking point and make it seem that there is no hope.* Start shoveling dirt in the pit to bury this battered and bleeding hero. *This is the low point, the point where we are now.*

Act Three: Surprise hero by making the crumbling dirt from above expose tree roots to create a ladder to climb out of dark pit. But if the hero had given up, he would never have seen this opportunity.

This is *why* we say, "It's always darkest before dawn." Because we sense or see the truth in it.

As any trained screenwriter knows, to craft a good story bad things must happen to the hero. But, as just explained, these "bad things" typically reach a crescendo at the very end of Act Two. You know, this is the point in the story where the well laid plan seemed to be going so well, but now all seems lost...

The hero has fought hard, but in vain it seems because the villain laid a trap or didn't die after all, game over. *If only* (here we go again) the hero had made a different choice or just stayed at home.

Would you judge the movie at this point?

No. Because *the story remains unfinished.*

The audience knows how the story will end: the hero will win (or they'll throw popcorn at the screen). But they sit on the edge of their seats regardless because they can't see *how* it will play out in the third and final act.

So they keep watching.

As must we.

Stay to the end. Let us not "walk out" of our own movie just when we're about to get to the good part.

Do you know many good stories that end with the hero throwing in the towel and so the bad guy wins?

Art and life are one and the same. The three-act story structure exists for a reason:

It's what it means to be human.

This is not the end. It's only the end of our Second Act. Our Third Act has begun and it's waiting for us to make a choice:

Option A: Go back. Return to how things were, stay in our comfort zone (of misery), and therefore continue to get more of the same. Or completely give up.

Option B: Bravely move forward and reforge our life, *whatever that may entail.*

Life is about making choices. Specifically, choosing between truth (however inconvenient) or ignorance. Sometimes the real problem isn't a wrong choice, but standing frozen between them.

Take Option B with me.

Don't walk out of your own movie.

Keep watching and let it play out to the end.

Act Three is where amazing things can happen *if our eyes are open to seeing them.*

Our final act is the first act of the rest of our lives.

The fire in my belly may have been drowned by sorrow, but at least now there was a spark. And a tiny spark is all it takes to conquer the mightiest castle.

I sprang to my feet, eyes wide. My photo album wasn't half-empty. It was half-*full*. And I could *choose* the photos that would fill the remaining pages. This time I would ensure it was the *right* photos.

I decided I would give myself the next seven days to reforge my life.

Give yourself the same.

DAY 2
WELCOME TO WHEREVER

Reset over regret

There is movement in stillness.

When a crisis hits, our instinct is to *do something*—to fix, to act, to fill the silence. But emotion is a poor navigator when raw.

So, let us pause and reset—long enough for truth to surface.

When we stop forcing outcomes, we create space for what was hidden to rise. The next step always shows itself to the one who understands the value of a reset.

The ancient Greeks warned what happens when the world forgets how to reset. When the goddess Persephone was abducted, her mother Demeter didn't weep in the corner—she shut down the planet. The changing seasons that agriculture needed to thrive suddenly stopped. No winter, so no renewal. No crops. No mercy...

No movement until I am heard.

The Sumerians called her Inanna. The Egyptians called her Isis. Every age remembers her differently, but her law is the same:

Destruction is the womb of creation.

Fire is not the end of life; it's the beginning of it. Every forest knows this. Every prairie. Every ancient goddess.

We forgot that. We built a culture afraid of endings, afraid to let anything die, even what poisons us. So, the dead wood piles up—habits, institutions, false identities, delusions—and when we block the burning, the fire comes for us anyway.

Enraged and unforgiving.

The task is not to avoid the fire but to master its rhythm. To make it sacred again. To stand in the clearing after the blaze and see the soil reborn, black and alive, smoke rising like prayer.

To *choose* reset over regret.

The remnants of the morning remained as I sat on my bed, the leather document pouch on one side of me and the photo album on the other. I flicked through the first few pages of the photo album. Baby pictures...

Innocence. Purity. Complete trust. No prejudice. New beginnings. An open book.

Gotta love babies.

I decided to walk to the park.

Alone, no phone.

I grabbed my document pouch and swung by the fish and chip shop on the way. There's something about a traditional fish and chip shop in Britain that can't be recreated anywhere else: the smell of lashings of malt vinegar cutting through salt and lard, the crisp paper it's wrapped in—a warming lunch parcel tucked under your arm.

I also ordered a slice of bread and butter so I could perform the classic British ceremony of feeding the ducks when I got to the park.

Walk with me.

Let's start by going back to the source of it all, right back to basics. The parts of my notes I still agreed with (and if we already know the basics, then how come more of us aren't following them?).

What brought us here?

What's stopping us from moving forward?

What stands between where we are and where we want to be?

Are we even sure we know where we want to be?

Whether we realize it or not, every human ultimately wants the same thing.

What is that one thing?

Happiness?

Close, but not quite.

What we're really after is inner peace (we assume happiness will give us inner peace—but peace is the root desire).

The dictionary calls it "a state of mental and emotional calmness, serenity, and freedom from stress, anxiety, or turmoil... a sense of balance and contentment even in the face of challenges."

Sounds about right.

Because whatever we chase—success, love, comfort, control—it's never really the thing itself we're after. It's the *feeling* we imagine it will bring.

We think, "Once I get there, I'll finally be at peace."

Everything from satisfying hunger to buying that shiny object to having that dream relationship to joining a protest march to making sorrow go away, the assumption is that it will bring us peace.

Or why would we pursue it?

Even the ugliest goals hide that same longing. From beating the Joneses to beating someone up, what we're really after is the same illusion of peace: "That'll show them. Then I'll finally relax."

But it never lasts, does it?

If you've ever "won" and felt that hollow quiet afterward, you know the truth: it's not peace—it's temporary sedation.

The chase resets, the craving returns.

"If I can just get that car, *then* I'll be at peace."

Nope.

"Okay, maybe if I get that job."

Nope.

"Maybe the perfect relationship."

Nope.

"Maybe leaving that relationship."

Still nope.

And on it goes. Like a donkey chasing a carrot on a stick.

Sadly, it often takes "having it all" or "losing it all" for us to finally hit the bloodstained brick wall of truth, with this message spray-painted across it:

"EVERYTHING YOU NEED ISN'T OUTSIDE YOU; IT'S *INSIDE* YOU."

If inner peace is the goal all humans share, whatever it is we wish we had, right now, the underlying assumption is that it will bring us peace. Therefore...

We can attain the ultimate goal of all humans here and now.

Why can't we cut out the middleman (the thing we assume will bring us peace) and head straight for the goal of inner peace? What's stopping us having inner peace right now?

In a word: *ourselves.*

Specifically, our minds. One of the most famous lines ever known starts to explain why:

"And God said, 'let there be light;' and there was light."

And so began the trouble.

That verse—Genesis 1:3—is the same scene portrayed in different ways throughout our most ancient texts and cultures across the world; a metaphor for the moment when humans "woke up" and separated from the rest of the animals, as humans received the blessing of consciousness (light is the classic symbol of consciousness).

The moment when we were able to *think*.

And the ability to think is both a blessing and a curse, for in the very next chapter of the Bible (and every other ancient text that preceded it) comes "the Fall," the expulsion from "Paradise;" the loss of the blissful ignorance all other animals enjoy.

Eden wasn't a place—it was a state of unbroken instinct. The fruit was consciousness, and we've been choking on its aftertaste ever since.

As Milton so aptly put it in *Paradise Lost:* "The mind is its own place and, in itself, can make a heaven of hell or a hell of heaven."

We can all relate to that, I am sure.

As Schopenhauer said about the Fall, "For to nothing does our existence bear so close a resemblance as to the consequence of a false step."

This is what Nietzsche was referring to when he said that humans are walking across a bridge over an abyss, a bridge away from being animals to where we need to be (an ultimate evolution goal he referred to as "Übermensch"), and we are not yet at the other side.

You see, the trouble is that this break away from the rest of the animal kingdom— caused by humans gaining the ability to think—wasn't a clean break. We were given a gift we still don't know how to handle.

The only "good" and "evil" in the world are our thoughts (and the subsequent realities that stem from them).

Marcus Aurelius was once emperor of the Roman Empire; he clearly 'had it all,' so he probably picked up a nugget or two of wisdom along the way. He said (emphasis mine), "Those who do not observe the movements of their own minds must *of necessity* be unhappy."

The ability to think is a mighty double-edged sword that must be mastered for it to become a powerful weapon used for good. An untrained mind cuts the one who wields it.

So let us train...

Stop the bleeding

Why is thinking a curse as well as a blessing?

Because we get what we focus on.

The human mind struggles to tell the difference between a thought and reality. This is why dreams feel completely real when we're in them.

So, when the brain has a *continual* thought, a good or bad vision, it will subconsciously home in on information that matches the thought as an attempt to make the physical world match our current view of the world. The thought becomes our reality (we will return to this idea in more detail on Day 7).

We have thousands of thoughts a day. And most of them are reruns.

Across time and geography, every tradition—east or west—warns us of the same thing: your thoughts are the world you live in (even if they typically only refer to males—a frustrating reality about ancient times that must not push us to discard the wisdom behind these texts. Kindly consider this as I quote them throughout the book):

The *Dhammapada* (Buddhism) says, "All that we are is a result of what we have thought." The *Bhagavad Gita* (Hinduism) says, "A person is what his shraddha (beliefs) are." The Bible says, "As a man thinketh in his heart, so is he."

Notice how the Bible does *not* say, "As a man is so shall he *think*." But we clearly aren't paying attention, are we? We usually let our current situation define our thoughts, and so we continually get more of the same in a never-ending downward spiral.

So, what are we supposed to do? Stop thinking?!

That would be like "trying to empty the ocean with a teacup," as Gandhi is attributed to saying.

This is the human condition: compulsive thinking.

The only solution, and the one we have no choice but to master, is this:

To be *mindful* of our thoughts.

It takes continual effort—and that's a pain in the ass, I know—but this mind of ours is like a young child; it can't be left unattended, or the house might burn down.

Left unattended, the mind usually defaults to the negative, which is one of humanity's biggest problems today. This is why we're more inclined to click on bad news headlines than good news headlines...

Out of fear.

For most of the 2.5 million years humans have existed, fear was useful for our survival. It kept us safe. In modern times (representing approximately only 0.008% of human existence!), it's keeping us in turmoil, limitation, and vulnerability.

Our minds are like old rivers flowing through new cities. You can take the human out of the stone age, but you can't take the stone age out of the human. At least, not without some effort.

Now let's apply this to our current distraught situation, which is one of worry, sorrow, and fear. In other words, those are our instinctive *thoughts* which are trying to keep us safe by making us remember the bad event so we don't do it again (like putting a hand in the fire).

But those thoughts—*complaints or fear about not being where we want to be*—are detailed, high-definition visions of the *future we are currently creating.*

So that needs to stop immediately.

We have to stop the bleeding before we do anything else.

In our present state, that's going to take some willpower and discipline. And the first step is for us to at least *attempt* to shut down *all* thinking for a while.

That's why we're alone now; no phone, in the park, feeding the ducks.

Enjoy the silence

I sat by a weeping willow beside the pond. The air was damp, the grass alive with dew. A fish broke the surface where my bread landed, then vanished again with a plop. A solitary magpie came and went like a messenger.

I gazed at the water, comparing it to our minds and the mission to make them still.

When we stop chasing, demanding, thinking, and complaining, solutions and paths will *come to us*. Our future currently consists of pure potential—multiple futures of unlimited possibility. But pure potential is often hidden from us without being in the void from which everything arises.

The mind merely executes what comes from a deeper place, the place we must return to now: a baby-like purity of thought.

Philosopher and scientist Blaise Pascal once made this profound statement: "All of man's troubles stem from his inability to sit quietly in a room alone."

All of our troubles!

Modern life isn't helping. Notice how there always has to be noise and background racket. TVs in bars, phones on speaker, "music" in elevators. I'm sure the writers of *A Quiet Place* (a movie where alien invaders kill anyone who makes a noise) shared this sentiment.

I don't think it's a coincidence that record levels of depression have come at the same time as record levels of stimulation. It's a simple but devastating chain reaction:

Overstimulation = overthinking = anxiety =
depression = suffering

As individuals and as a species, we must break this chain.

The Tao says, "To clarify muddy waters, you must hold them still and let things settle... In returning to the root, we find tranquility; this leads to our destiny..."

The mind is a bit like a pond when you look at it with the goal of making it still. On the surface is all the falling debris, weather, noise, and waves, like the daily noise, chatter, and overstimulation we experience.

But imagine now going deeper under the water. The noise fades, the water becomes still, and all we can hear is our breathing as we hit the bottom, like a pebble swaying downwards to its resting place. If you've ever tried meditation, it's a similar process. It's bringing the mind home—like rain returning to the ocean that made it.

Silence is the sound of our spirit regrouping.

Whenever you've been in a situation where your thoughts shut down and you were forced to be present, your senses were heightened. This is because you were in a state of "no mind."

This same state of heightened awareness allows us to tap into a source more powerful and constructive than anything the mind could come up with.

Perhaps you've noticed this in a sport or when creating art. Training can get too mechanical, detaching us from our incredible, instinctive powers that come from deep within and surprise us...

... as if a "hidden hand" did it...

... and as if time hadn't existed during the event...

We'll look at what's behind that on Day 7. For now, let's understand that time is the mind's ally. The past, the future, time, time, time. Notice how young children struggle with the concept of "tomorrow" and "yesterday." They have to learn it.

Take away the concept of time—of past and future—leaving only the present, and doesn't the thing making us sad also disappear?

Suffering ceases in the present because suffering needs the concept of time to survive.

But even with all these stillness strategies, I *know* that one highly destructive thought (i.e. *a future vision we keep creating*) is the most reluctant of them all to leave us alone. And with it, one question still lingers:

How do we resist the temptation to constantly replay our crisis and wish things had been different?

The power of surrender

> *"Lead me, fate, wherever you will,*
> *And I will cheerfully follow.*
> *For, even if I kick and wail,*
> *All the same I must follow."*
> —Cleanthes

The first step to escaping a prison is to accept that you are in prison.

This means surrendering to what *is*. It does not mean we are giving up trying to get *out* of the prison. It means we are not *resisting* the fact that we're in one *right now*.

There is a profound difference between surrender and giving up.

We're like ships straining for the horizon, blind to the fact that the tide decides the timing. And the tide itself bows to the moon.

But we don't abandon the journey; we observe the tides.

We surrender.

Have you ever noticed how when you chase something you want desperately that it continually slips out of reach? But when you stop trying so hard, when you back off and go do something else, you get what you wanted, right?

Notice how you didn't give up. You didn't stop wanting it.

In effect, perhaps without realizing, you simply *surrendered*. You stopped trying to force the hand of fate. It's like the proverbial couple who can't conceive a baby, so they adopt a baby instead, and then she gets pregnant. It's finding love in the supermarket instead of the singles bar.

When we look back on the medieval monks who ritually flailed themselves, it's easy for us moderns to scratch our heads or laugh. But their sentiment comes from this same place of humility and surrender. This idea—the subjugation of the mind's will—was also central to the philosophies of Schopenhauer.

Walking to the other side of the park, to the edge of a river (and almost slipping into the water) I recalled a line from Alan Watts: "When you try to stay on the surface of the water, you sink; but when you try to sink, you float."

Fate is like the flowing current of the river I stood beside. It's moving, with you or without you, so it may as well be with you. Roman philosopher Seneca saw it the same way: "Fate leads the willing and drags along the reluctant."

Practical safety protocol agrees. If you fall into a fast-moving river with a strong current, do not resist the flow, *go with it*, and steadily ease yourself over to the bank to get out.

Watch a river flow. Watch how it continually surrenders to obstructions and yet remains steady on its course. Power from pliability. This is why the properties of water are a central part of the Tao.

The mind wants certainty, a sure thing. We want life to have guarantees, like when we buy a toaster. But other than death and taxes, there is only one thing that's truly guaranteed:

Change.

Count on it.

In the park, I saw how winter had stripped the trees of their former glory, made them bare and menacing, but who would wish for them to be hacked down? To wish for life without change is to wish for life without nature. And there cannot be life without nature.

Loss is simply change. And nature delights in change. We cannot fear nature because we *are* nature:

Humans = Nature = Change

This is the reality. The fantasy is how our mind wants to perceive it (and resist it).

By *definition*, the mind only perceives. It's all a matter of opinion. As Proust said, "The universe is true for us all and dissimilar to each of us."

Here's an example:

Have you noticed how the vision of ourselves in the mirror doesn't usually match a photograph of us (however much we turn our heads and suck in our cheeks)? I witness this phenomenon myself all the time:

Reaction when looking in mirror: "I'm looking good for my age."

Reaction when looking at photograph: "Alexa, search for plastic surgeons near me!"

In other words, there is a mismatch between our perception and reality. Our eyes don't deceive us; the mind does by its interpretation of the image our eyes are projecting *into* our minds (the eye is mostly just a lens, like a camera).

The mind is biased.

A famous experiment proved this when a group of people were told to watch a video of people passing a ball to each other and to count the number of people wearing white shirts as opposed to black shirts. Meanwhile, a person dressed in a gorilla suit walked right across the set, plain as day. After watching the video the group was asked if they saw a gorilla. Most of them said they didn't until they rewatched the video, when they were *looking* for a gorilla.

Right now, it may *feel* like there's no way out of this hole, no light at the end of this tunnel, but the operative word here is "feel." It's only what we *perceive* as being the case...

But we aren't yet noticing that "gorilla" in the room.

A curious thing about the mind, probably as an ancient survival mechanism, is that once it develops a hard opinion about something it typically only sees information that backs up this opinion. As I said, it is biased...

Specifically, the mind suffers from something called "confirmation bias;" *it only sees things that confirm its opinion.*

So if our mind's current opinion is something like, "I am in pain," "I am a loser," "I will never come back from this," "I can't go on without him," etc. we will only see information that backs this up, and a self-reinforcing downward spiral takes hold as we stray into a synthetic nightmare we believe to be our reality.

Meanwhile, the world is still turning, the waves are still crashing, and the birds are still singing.

So, we don't experience life as much as perceive it, and right now our *perception* is darkness.

And that must change.

We aren't sweeping struggle under the rug; we are changing our *opinion* of it.

Circumstances are neutral. The ultimate and universal goal of inner peace cannot be stolen by circumstance. Only our mind can do that.

I don't want to discount what's happened to us, only our opinion of it, to assist in the process of surrender. Because resistance to struggle only amplifies the pain. Wanting to get out of struggle *is* struggle.

So, what if we could become indifferent to the pleasure-pain cycle, and merely witness it? To become the "undimmed mirror of the world" that Schopenhauer wrote of.

From the *Bhagavad Gita*: "Those who are unaffected by these changes, who are the same in pleasure and pain, are truly wise and fit for immortality."

The concept of "The Wheel of Fortune" began in Rome, but was popularized in the Middle Ages, where the advice was to stay in the hub of the wheel—the center—so one would be immune to the inevitable ups and downs of fortune as the wheel turned.

In Holy Grail legend, it was said that the Grail was brought to Earth from Heaven by *neutral* angels who favored neither God nor Satan.

We've never ignored that wisdom more than we do now...

Humans have never tried so hard to take the "bitter" out of "bittersweet," and they have never been so unhappy.

When we see that the concepts of "good" and "bad" are one and the same, we escape the concept of "good" and "bad." And our minds labeling our current situation as "good" or "bad" is what creates our perception, and therefore our reality.

Let's shift that perception before we go any further.

Reinventing redemption

Humans came from the Earth. Earth came from the Universe. This means humans are the grandchildren—the direct descendants—of the Universe.

We literally *are* the Universe.

Something science has observed about the Universe is that it is constantly expanding at a terrifying rate. In other words, it wants change, renewal, and *creative destruction*.

Which means deep down, we want the same thing.

Rise and fall, fall and rise—a circular dance; this is the natural order of things.

Goethe agreed: "Shaping, reshaping. The eternal spirit's eternal pastime."

We have been offered this advice for thousands of years in different ways at different times, but something along the way got lost.

The Sumerians called her Inanna, the Egyptians called her Isis, the Greeks called her Demeter... and today we call her Mary.

***True* compassion is not the denial of endings. It's the courage to allow them.**

Because Demeter's abducted daughter—Persephone—always returns in Spring.

These reminders of the basics helped me to settle and shift my perspective. Some uncertainty remained and being honest, perhaps a dash of dread and loneliness. But now I was ready for the next step. And a new playbook.

In the park, the wind rustling the bushes and the moon challenging the fading sun prompted me to head back to my cave. My mother would have a hot meal waiting.

On the way back I walked up a hill to employ a trick learned from years of being an airline pilot that helps us quickly adapt to new time zones.

It involves changing the mind's opinion of when sunrise and sunset happen by simply watching the sun set (and rise). You're telling the mind what's happening instead of it telling you.

As we said, it's all about perspective, and very often that perspective is false. Even our perspective that the sun is "going *down*" is false.

The sun never "goes down."

Think about it from the Universe's perspective; how it's the Earth that orbits the sun and rotates on its axis. The sun isn't setting.

It's *us* who are *rising*.

"Do you hear me?" I said to the sky. "*We are rising!*"

DAY 3

DELETED SCENES

Cut!

What would *Psycho* be without the shower scene?

When Alfred Hitchcock released his masterpiece in 1960, people in audiences fainted, ran out of theaters screaming, and some even sought therapy afterward. None of that would have happened without the shower scene. Without it, *Psycho* might still have been a clever thriller—but it would not have become a cultural shockwave.

To this day, people still pull back shower curtains in hotel bathrooms, often without realizing why. That reflex—that tiny jolt of checking the unseen—comes directly from Hitchcock's iconic scene. The scene rewired cultural muscle memory. It also influenced a generation of young filmmakers. Spielberg, after studying Hitchcock shot-by-shot, later used the same recipe to terrify people with *Jaws*.

Even modern theater etiquette owes something to *Psycho*. The idea that you shouldn't enter after a film begins was Hitchcock's invention; he wanted audiences sealed in, nowhere to run, trapped inside the experience he'd engineered.

And of course, something even bigger began there: modern horror. Before *Psycho*, horror was gothic, supernatural, or camp. After *Psycho*, horror became psychological and terrifyingly close to home.

And yet, the shower scene almost didn't exist.

Compared to today, 1960 was a safe and sterile culture. Hitchcock even had to fight the censor board to show a flushing toilet in the film, so imagine the look on their faces when he explained the film would feature a man dressed in his mother's clothes who stabs a naked woman to death in the shower! The studio also refused to fund the picture, mostly because of that one scene.

But Hitchcock wouldn't back down. His shower scene would not be deleted from the script. He had to come up with a way to make the movie complete.

First, he decided to mortgage his house and fund the movie himself—a huge gamble. To save money he would film it in black-and-white. Getting it past the censor board was a bigger challenge, though, and would require ingenuity. So he devised a cunning plan that would also go on to make his work so influential.

Hitchcock understood the human condition and how to manipulate it. He didn't care about gore—all he cared about was mind-state. He, and later Spielberg, played on a primal secret of human psychology:

Horror is what the audience *imagines* just outside the frame. Fear is created by anticipation, not depiction. In other words...

Fear and tension are created by what we *don't* see.

Like Hitchcock, each of us needs to fight for a crucial scene not to be deleted—*however horrific it might be.*

Except our fight is an internal one. A scene was deleted from the story of our *lives*.

Pause, rewind

On Day One we talked about writing the third act of our life movie —the final and greatest act, right? Before we do, though, let's pause and rewind...

Right to the beginning.

Okay. Now press play, and let's watch Act One of your life. You may *think* you know what's there, but let's take a closer look.

You sit back and watch, studying every detail of every scene...

And then you see it.

Or rather, you *don't* see it:

An entire scene has been deleted.

Remember on Day One how I said a story typically begins with something like the hero being thrown into a dark pit? That's the classic Act One set up. It's what screenwriters call the "inciting incident;" a point of no return, a problem that puts pressure on the hero to resolve it.

Well, yours is missing. It's like nothing bad happened.

Your inciting incident has been deleted.

Not much of a movie without one, is it? It wouldn't make any sense, for starters.

Perhaps this is why so many of us feel our lives don't make sense.

What happened? Who deleted that scene, and why?

Your inner "censor board" deemed that scene too scary for Act One, the earliest years of your life. And it was *right* to do so—your barely formed psyche in your fragile years wouldn't have been able to handle it.

But you're not a kid anymore.

Not that the censor board cares about that.

The good news is that scene was only deleted from the story that plays out in your mind (even if something feels off about it). It wasn't lost; it was merely cut out by the "censor board."

Better still, you also have an inner "director" who won't put up with that omission anymore.

But this director couldn't leave that part of Act One blank. Its job is to keep the audience (you) entertained somehow. So it filled that gap in the reel with something it made up until you were old enough to process the original scene.

As we grow older the director tires of the bullshit. It's coming for the deleted scene even if it means defying the censor board. The director wants final cut (and we all know the "director's cut" is the coolest).

In biological shorthand:

"Censor board" = the defensive network

"Director" = the executive network

"Deleted Scene" = dissociated memory

When something overwhelming happens early in life, the brain doesn't record it like a normal memory. It records it as survival data.

The defensive network ("censor board") decides whether an experience is "safe enough" to store or "too dangerous" to let into conscious memory. If the event is too intense for a child's developing system, it sounds the alarm.

It rates it "M: Mature audiences only."

In those early years, the executive network ("director") is not yet mature enough to process what's happening.

So the experience gets stored in scattered fragments—sensations, emotions, flashbacks, dreams—but not as a coherent story you can easily recall.

Later in life, the executive network ("director") grows up and tries to create a coherent narrative of who you are and why you behave the way you do. But it can't find the full scene, because it was never encoded properly, it was deliberately buried. It's like having forced amnesia.

So you end up with:

1. **a defensive network holding the raw, unprocessed intensity,**

2. **an executive network trying to direct your life story without an inciting incident.**

So when you move toward any action that resembles the context of that early event—risk, exposure, change, standing up, being seen—the defensive network automatically activates the old shutdown pattern.

Your body says, "don't move," even though your adult mind wants to.

This is not a psychological weakness. It's not a lack of discipline. It's not a fear of failure. It's biology doing exactly what it was designed to do: protect you from an experience you never finished processing.

And this is exactly why mainstream self-help doesn't work for so many people.

Self-help speaks to the executive network—the part that makes plans, sets goals, and tells stories. But the problem isn't happening there...

The shutdown lives in the defensive network, which doesn't understand motivational speeches, reason, "go get em" discipline, changing habits, or vision boards.

It understands survival.

So self-help keeps giving you cognitive tools for a non-cognitive problem. It keeps trying to coach the "director" while the "censor" is the one calling the shots.

That's why you can read all the books, do all the exercises, have all the best intentions, and still feel stuck: *the advice never reaches the part of you that's actually stopping you getting started.*

So don't blame yourself.

That is, unless you *now* refuse the call to attend to unfinished business.

The defensive network does respond to something other than survival. It also understands patterns, emotions, and meaning.

Which means it also responds to stories. And that is one reason why our myths exist.

"Story" is what the defensive network is censoring, after all.

Ancient people didn't have the benefit of biology to explain things, but they sensed the same inner drama we all do and wove the universal truth of the "deleted scene" into their storytelling:

- Orpheus descending to the Underworld
- Inanna descending through the gates
- Psyche completing impossible tasks
- Odysseus meeting the dead
- Jesus descending before rising

Those myths are metaphors for the necessary inner journey that's as old as the hills:

The journey into the part of the self that got sealed off. The retrieval of what the conscious mind cannot readily access. The reclamation of lost memory, agency, truth, and identity.

In Viking mythology, Odin is the god who pursues truth at any cost.

His journey leads him to Mímir's Well, a deep spring of memory and forbidden knowledge located beneath one of the roots of Yggdrasil, the World Tree (does a tree of "forbidden knowledge" sound familiar?).

That root reaches down toward "Hel," the Viking underworld—the realm of what is buried, forgotten, repressed, or cut off from the living world.

Because of its position near Hel's domain, Mímir's Well holds not surface knowledge but the deep truth, the kind that lies below consciousness.

Guarding the well is Mímir, who demands a price from anyone seeking to see what lies beneath the ordinary mind.

Odin asks for a drink from the well.

Mímir refuses until Odin pays what the well requires.

Odin accepts. He removes one eye and drops it into the well (a sacrifice of outer sight so he can gain *inner* sight into what the psyche normally hides). Only then is he allowed to drink.

What Odin receives is not comforting illumination; it is the truth from the realm near Hel—intense, ancestral, shadowed knowledge.

This drink grants him insight into things no one else can bear to see: fate, death, trauma, the coming apocalypse.

Odin's lost eye remains forever at the bottom of Mímir's Well, gazing up from the darkness of Hel's border. It symbolizes the permanent cost of confronting buried truth:

You cannot see the world the same way again once you retrieve what was hidden.

That word—*apocalypse*—didn't originally mean fire or destruction. In Greek, *apokalypsis* meant *"lifting of the veil,"* the moment when something hidden is finally revealed.

That's exactly what happens when you confront your own deleted scene. It isn't the end of your world; it's the end of not knowing. Once the veil lifts, you can't go back to the old story or the old blindness.

Like Odin's eye at the bottom of the well, the truth stays with you. It changes how you see everything.

After a deep sleep, I woke up late on that third day—a Wednesday. Sitting up in bed, sipping a cup of tea, I flicked through the next pages of my photo album: first day of school and birthday parties. Happy, happy.

After a welcome shower and claiming a second "cuppa," I sat down for the classic British Breakfast: flame-grilled tomato, seared mushrooms, baked beans, two fried eggs, two crisped British bacon rashers, two bangers, and lashings of HP brown sauce; its distinctively piquant kick balancing it all. And as if all that isn't enough to kill you, the commonly expected side of toast is replaced with fried bread. Flashbacks to thinking I was dying of a heart attack last week.

My mother had planned the week out for me, but I respectfully told her I had my own plans now. I had my reasons.

Borrowing her car, I planned to drive into town—closer to where I spent my earliest years—to visit an old movie theater I used to frequent as a child.

Stepping outside, I embraced a clear and bitterly cold morning as I gazed up at the blue. A plane at high altitude slashed the sky with its twinned white vapor trails.

I got in the car and started the engine. The *Hits from the Seventies!* radio station burst into life—halfway through Led Zeppelin singing *Immigrant Song*. I stamped on the clutch, rammed into gear, and peeled away.

Come along for the ride. And buckle up.

Exorcising is not healthy

Some might say, "Leave the past where it is! Don't open old wounds! It serves no purpose anymore, let it go! It's hurting people's feelings! It's scaring me...!"

A relatively small group of extremely vocal but well-intended people try to protect us from the flame of reality, trying to sterilize the world, acting like the "censor board," not appreciating how weak their actions make us, stunting our growth, depriving us of our rite of passage.

But if we were never exposed to germs and viruses we would never develop any immunity, we would never become strong. It's the same principle.

Most people fight their darkness.

And most people lose but have the illusion of winning.

We can surround ourselves with white picket fences, we can barricade our front doors and pray the darkness won't overrun our mental defenses, but...

Look around. Look backstage of the big social play people act in. How's that working out for us? Behind the social media scenes of playtime perfection it's digital enslavement, addictions, depression, indifference, annihilation, and this creeping horror is getting steadily worse...

We're being eaten alive.

The darkness doesn't even need to overcome our puny defenses *because we took it with us... it's inside us.* It's part of who we are, but we are neglecting its plea because something inside us tells us we're being defiant to do so.

Unless confronted, these memories cast a silent shadow that stretches into the present, warping your decisions without you knowing, whispering in your ear, and pulling the strings.

When a dissociated memory isn't integrated into consciousness, the psyche does what humans have always done when faced with overwhelming inner material: *it turns the internal into the external.*

That's the danger. Not just to the individual, but *society at large.* School shootings are just one of the many tragic casualties that litter the news headlines.

Externalizing the internal drama was also the root of the belief in possession and exorcism...

Before we had trauma theory or even the concept of the unconscious, cultures that lost the metaphor of myth interpreted dissociated states as possession, bewitchment, or "hysteria." The Salem witch trials were mass projection—collective panic trying to expel what it couldn't confront internally.

Victorian doctors treated women with what we now recognize as dissociation using "hysteria cures" involving pelvic massage—and some even adopted early electro-mechanical massage devices, the direct precursors to modern vibrators, to speed up the process.

In modern research, untreated dissociated memories *map almost one-to-one* with the same outcomes as what we once thought was demonic possession.

Every era names the deleted scene differently, but the pattern never changes. When the psyche can't integrate what happened, it mythologizes it, pathologizes it, or *demonizes it.*

Call it a demon, a witch, hysteria, or a "lack of discipline" —the result is the same. Unseen footage takes control until you finally turn inward and lift the veil yourself.

Jung explained that what I call deleted scenes "are vulnerable points which we do not like to remember and still less like to be reminded of by others **but also as a stimulus to greater effort...**"

A big weakness can be reforged into a big strength. Weakness is just energy trapped in the wrong form. Energy cannot be destroyed, but it can change form.

When you repurpose that energy it's no longer a liability; it's raw fuel for transformation. Through mastery, repetition, and adaptation, it becomes power...

Fear becomes awareness and precision.

Anger becomes drive and execution.

Overthinking becomes depth and mastery.

So, you either face it, or it runs your life from the dark.

Echoing Viking myth somewhat, Nietzsche said, "The tree that would grow to heaven must send its roots to hell." Jung agreed: "Until you make the unconscious conscious, it will direct your life and you will call it fate... Drink down all of what we have held at a distance in order to grow."

So, go to hell.

Hell isn't outside you. It's inside you. And there's only one way out: *through*.

I'm reminded of that famous scene in *Lawrence of Arabia* where Lawrence extinguishes a lit match with his fingers and doesn't show any sign of pain. A fellow officer, William Potter, tries to do the same and fails, fanning his burned finger.

"Ooh! It damn well hurts!" Potter says.

Lawrence replies, "Certainly it hurts."

Potter asks, "What's the trick, then?"

"The trick, William Potter...is not *minding* that it hurts."

A picture of the past

I didn't tell you I was going to see my father on the way to the theater. Perhaps I didn't want to.

My palms grew a little sweaty on the steering wheel. My chest felt constricted. I was driving a stick-shift on tight and winding roads I was no longer familiar with.

The rearview mirror was missing. My mother's car was kept exactly as it always was, unchanged since my childhood: a dumpster on wheels, crap everywhere (and I'm OCD tidy). It felt like a prison.

And it wasn't helping that I couldn't figure out how to change the damned radio station—it seemed to be locked on *Hits from the 70s!* Then *The Chain* by Fleetwood Mac played, and suddenly I was back there...

London Borough of Hounslow, 1977. My mother was a hippie trapped in a soccer-mom's body.

I didn't always know where the next meal was coming from, and getting a packed lunch was sometimes hit-or-miss, but she loved me dearly. And there was no limit to her agreeing to take me, her seven-year-old, to the movie theater to watch this zany new film called *Star Wars*.

On that fresh autumn morning, through hastily applied lipstick bordered by sweeping blonde hair, she lamented how sadly ironic it was that rock icon, Marc Bolan of *T. Rex*, was terrified of cars, and yet he had just died in a car crash the other night.

All this as I sat on the front seat of her car-cum-dumpster without a seat belt. Our trusty German Shepherd had been named Marc as a tribute to the now-dead rock star, and he occupied the rear seat next to my baby sister, his proud head pushed out the semi-lowered window, anticipating the rush of scented air.

Our Vauxhall Viva station wagon bounced off the driveway as we playfully nodded our heads to Fleetwood Mac, headed to school in a leafy London suburb for my first day of second grade, as we both sang out of tune.

At drop-off, she kissed me goodbye and, as I marched through the school gate, she said *The Force* would be with me. Always. I tapped my right temple with my forefinger, in response.

As I mentally mapped my assault on the "Death Star," a giant with red lipstick ushered me to my classroom, and introduced me to my new teacher, Mrs. Kendall. Wide-eyed, perched on my wooden chair, I awaited my briefing, R2-D2 pencil at the ready.

Mrs. Kendall appeared to be a kind, elderly lady with oval-shaped rose-colored glasses, and she addressed her new class as if it was the opening ceremony of The Olympic Games.

Her first order of business was to set the ground rules, and she'd engineered a sly Pavlovian system to control us. Pointing to the top shelf in the open closet to the right of her desk, she said there was a powerful, magical wizard up there watching us all.

She referred to a six-inch doll dressed in a wizard's outfit. This wizard guarded a jar of merrily colored candy.

She continued ominously, explaining that we would each receive a candy from this wizard on the Friday of each week *if we'd been well behaved.*

But she was the only one who could hear or speak to The Wizard, she said.

Getting the candy wasn't my priority. What I wanted most was a private audience with The Wizard without *her* as the middleman. To hell with that bullshit.

This was because of something that had happened recently...

My father loved me; it just didn't seem that way. On the times he whacked me across the face, it somehow felt like more than just a punishment for whatever I'd done wrong; it seemed like retribution for something. And I seemed to do a lot of things wrong.

In the previous year, the school gave me a special award for creative writing, but when I showed it to him he tossed it to one side, and told me I couldn't become a success doing something like writing. He always said I would "never be successful" for one reason or another.

I'd try to keep out of his way by staying with my maternal grandparents as much as possible, watching airplanes land at Heathrow Airport from their backyard, sharing my grandfather's binoculars, as he told me old aviation stories from when he was a radio engineer. It was like having two sets of parents.

Weekdays made it hard to escape from home because of school, and, on one such weekday night, I overheard my parents screaming at each other. He was yelling about her never having dinner ready when he got home, never knowing where she was.

And then I heard it for the first time—my real name—according to him: *Useless Eustis*.

Like it had always been true. Like I had been called it a thousand times before. From birth.

Then my father pushed my mother out the front door and locked it, leaving her crying in the rain. I ran downstairs to the door to let her back in, but angry claws jammed into my ribs, yanked me away, and hurled me onto a chair.

I really wanted that private audience with The Wizard.

After a couple of weeks at school, I'd finally figured out the weakness in Mrs. Kendall's defenses: it appeared The Wizard was only watching us on Fridays. You could've peed against the old dear's desk Monday through Thursday, but provided you were a "little angel" on the Friday, you were golden for that candy.

So if I wanted a one-on-one with The Wizard I would need to make my move on a Friday, as that appeared to be the only day he could hear us. And today was a Friday, so it was go-time.

I waited until the other kids were milling around between crayon tables so I could use them as cover, then I deftly crept towards The Wizard, one eye on Kendall working at her desk.

My X-wing fighter maneuvered down the Death Star trench, the film's soundtrack playing in my head...

"...stay on target, Red 5, *stay on target*... preparing to fire torpedoes...

... wait, TIE fighters coming in, six o'clock...!"

Kendall craned her neck around at me.

"They... came from... be-hind...!"

"Divert all power to rear deflector shields!"

My "shields:" My paternal grandparents once told me that I had a demonic face I'd pull when being denied something. 'The Face' once made a passing driver slam on his brakes in horror, almost crashing— "James! Stop that!" she yelled as she slapped the back of my head and asked if I could please never show The Face again.

Before Kendall's mouth could open, I threw her The Face, my unspoken words: "Back off, sister, I'm trying to speak to the boss man, here!"

Spooked, right on cue, she slowly turned away, as if to pacify a wild animal she'd stumbled into.

"You're all clear, kid, now let's blow this thing and go home!" I heard Han Solo say.

Alone with The Wizard, at last, I held my offering up to him: a crayoned self-portrait of my future; a man dressed in a black suit and tie, standing next to a table of gold coins.

He was a millionaire.

I slid the picture into the bottom shelf of The Wizard's closet.

I figured I was the cause of my mommy getting locked out—because I had been "useless" instead of "successful"—so I closed my eyes tightly and crushed my hands together.

Now I could say my prayer:

"Dear Wizard, please make me successful, please make me successful. Not useless. Thank you, thank you."

"And so it happens that many a man carries round throughout his life a burden of absurd notions, whims, crotchets, fancies, and prejudices that ultimately become fixed ideas," said Schopenhauer.

There are far worse childhood experiences than that, but it's the only one I've got. This isn't a pissing contest about who has the most M-rated deleted scene; it's about putting our movie back together. The principle is the same, regardless of intensity.

I pulled into the long driveway of a mansion that had been converted into a nursing home, tires crunching over gravel. I switched off the engine and stared at the entrance to the building, ivy clinging to one side of it.

I hadn't seen my father for many years. It must have been at my nephew's christening over ten years ago—when I threw a punch at him and walked out. He had been financially crippled at the time, and I relished the opportunity to tell him he was "useless" as his body flew back from the blow.

In the decade since we had barely spoken. During my absence he had mentally deteriorated from alcohol abuse and slowly drank himself into this place in his mid-sixties. When faced with his own major life-crisis he had climbed inside a bottle of cognac and never came out.

He walked out of his own movie right at the end of its second act.

None of that assured me that day, feeling like a seven-year-old child walking up those steps. Especially now that I was going through my own crisis. Now that *I* had been so close—only last week—to doing exactly what he had done.

I imagined him waiting for me inside, gloating at *Useless Eustis*.

As I entered the building, it hit me that this really was a nursing home. That smell: a blend of soup and urine. The heating turned up too high.

An orderly escorted me along a narrow corridor to a doorway on the right. I peered my head around the threshold, and there he was:

A wounded and starving lion.

His body was frail, his eyes sunken and confused. A skull with chalky skin attached.

Then I saw it. Not in his words, not in his face, but in his eyes— nothing. He had no clue who I was.

I sat opposite him. "Hi, Dad."

"Hell—*o*," he said, like a kind stranger, eyes wide with curiosity about me.

A tear burned its way up before I could stop it. And then—fuck—it was out there.

He watched the tear fall. And then, only for a split-second that I didn't imagine, I saw a flicker of light in his eyes as he read me in that way only a concerned parent can.

"It'll be okay," he said.

An involuntary gulp squeezed out a second tear, and my faculties jammed, I couldn't find the words, only a thought:

I wish I could talk to you right now, Dad. More than ever.

But then he was gone again.

Whatever demons possessed him in the past had left him years ago.

And now mine had left, too.

Now let's see what's been hiding behind the "shower curtain" of *your* mind.

Treat this next part as a sacred ritual. Nobody is allowed in your inner theater once the show starts...

Pull back the curtain

The lights go out, we're in darkness.

The curtains open...

See it.

That moment you never talk about. The scene that got cut because it didn't serve the story...

If it doesn't hurt you're looking at the wrong scene.

You know exactly what it is...

When it is...

Where it is...

We're watching that deleted scene together now. Front row seats. You and me.

It's one of your earliest memories.

Watch...

Don't filter it.

Don't explain.

Watch and hear the whole scene play out, and save any judgments about it until it's over. You aren't reading a book now; you're immersing yourself in an experience.

We're not going to rewrite it or deny it—the "censor board" has already done that. We'd be no better off.

Just watch and witness the whole scene.

It happened.

What's happening to that child actor in this scene...?

Beaten into conformity? Saying they're useless? Ordered to be silent? Being abandoned? Shamed? Abused? Threats?

All of the above?

Read all the actors' lines in this scene.

Out loud.

Right now. (No one will hear you. But you will.)

Read.

And watch...

Don't continue until you've seen it *in full*.

Has your deleted scene played out?

Well done.

Let's now rewind and watch the slow-motion replay...

Can you see that?

Something feels off...

The actors on that stage are reading their lines—the lines you know so well—but...

... the lines are spoken, the movements are precise—*too precise*—like they've done this a thousand times before.

And they have. This scene runs daily down here. The actors seem jaded and tired.

Who wrote this screenplay?

Who wrote your character's lines?

Who wrote the lines of the character who's oppressing that child?

The actors are the puppets. Who was pulling their strings?

Has the scene fully finished?

Okay.

Now it's our turn.

I want you to now visualize this:

Next, something extraordinary happens...

The scene pauses. Freeze-frame.

Then a trapdoor on the stage beneath the screen opens, revealing a staircase that goes underneath and behind the screen. This staircase divides the child actor from the actor playing the oppressor. Smoke and ash fly out of the open trapdoor. You feel the heat.

Both actors suddenly look at you sitting in the audience.

Then *I* look at you.

Now, I want you to walk onto the stage, take the child by the hand, and take it down those stairs...

To the fire!

Not to destroy. To *reforge*.

See it! You walk onto the stage; you take the child by the hand.

The child doesn't resist; it just looks up at you and smiles.

The other person in this scene is powerless, their jaw hits the floor, as you walk this relieved child down the trapdoor, down the stairs, into the fire.

The flames rise to meet you both, but neither of you flinches. You step into them, and they don't scorch. They clear away the layers, the masks.

There's no turning back, no safety net. What's left is *pure you*—raw, unstoppable, free.

You don't burn in the fire.

Because you have become the fire.

As you walk through the flames, you remain unscathed, but the child melts away, smiling wider than before... at peace, free at last...

But as you look closer, all that's melting away from the child is the shame, guilt, and doubt, a purging... the child is becoming reforged... and *merging into your body.*

The heat has melded this deleted scene back into your life-movie.

We haven't changed the past, only your relationship to it.

The movie now plays on, complete and true.

Carry out the ritual as many times as necessary—until you see this deleted scene for exactly what it is: a tired script with lousy actors that has run its course.

That child must be burned and reforged back into your psyche, its trapped energy harnessed. Not abandoned here in this terrible place; imprisoned in this eternally looping scene.

If this place feels like hell, then the only "sin" you're here for is defying the "censor board."

Long before "sin" became moral or religious, it pointed to something older and far more human: the break from the tribe. In the oldest mythic patterns, the first "wrong" isn't guilt or "missing the mark"— it's the moment a human steps out of the collective tribal mind and feels the first spark of a separate self.

That rupture, that first flicker of "I," was the *original* "sin."

Backstage pass

Fractured things eventually crack up.

Including us.

We are the unsuspecting prisoners of a survival mechanism that's not required in adulthood.

It wasn't malicious. We must give thanks to the "censor board" for its care in those early years. And it will always be around—its voice is what you'll hear whenever you're tempted back to stagnation and sterility, whenever you feel resistance to personal growth, and whenever the weak and needy side of us cries for someone to make the pain magically go away.

Norman Bates—and the *real* killer who inspired the book the movie was based on, Ed Gein—grew up under mothers so controlling, so engulfing, that their inner "directors" never developed enough to stand up to the "censor board." Add severe childhood trauma on top of that, and you get a mind full of deleted scenes with no executive system strong enough to reintegrate them.

That's how we create *true* monsters. Only by shining a light "under the bed" are monsters defeated.

The deleted scene is just a memory. The only reality it has is the meaning you give it in the present. When you pull back the shower curtain, when you realize that the inner tension was about what we *couldn't* see, the illusion is exhausted.

Hitchcock resolved his problem in a similar way. He didn't defeat the censors head-on. He outflanked them.

He shot the shower scene with over 70 camera setups and 52 rapid cuts—a three minute scene that took a whole week to film. Not a single frame showed the knife penetrating skin. Not one shot showed actress Janet Leigh nude in a way the censors prohibited. Every "stab" was an illusion built from fast cuts to interrupt visual continuity—oblique angles that suggested violence without displaying it, knife glints timed with musical "shrieks," body doubles shot only in fragments, and screams laid over shots of nothing more than tiles and chocolate syrup draining down a plughole.

The human mind filled in the blanks—that's where the true horror lived.

The censors watched the final cut and were furious at what seemed like blatant defiance—certain they had seen nudity and graphic murder.

Hitchcock calmly replied, "Show me the frame."

They couldn't. Because there wasn't one.

By the way, *our* hero "director" who defied the "censor board" has a name you're probably more familiar with:

"Ego."

Hits from the 70s! wasn't so bad. Marc Bolan sang *Cosmic Dancer* to me from beyond the grave—on the radio as I drove back. It sounded like a ghostly goodbye waltz, the road humming along.

I decided to rent a car the next day, but I'd adapted into using the two wing-mirrors in the absence of a rearview mirror. Driving toward sunset illuminated everything behind me. *Objects in mirror are closer than they appear.* Truly.

I let the weight of the day settle in. And I made declarations I would do my best to adhere to.

I would no longer be bound by the need to prove, justify, or react defensively. I would engender a presence beyond fear, and no longer be chained to what no longer served me: "Don't get close to anyone.

Nobody can be trusted. Leave them before they leave you."

But that was behind me. And I would deal with my own reckoning — for anyone else's deleted scene I star in—with grace and unconditional submission to their truth, when and if that day came.

Useless Eustis died in the flames that day. He was always meant to be burned—*and reintegrated*. But I didn't die. I came back to life with renewed verve. And a newfound clarity.

It was dark when I arrived back at my mother's house, and the shadows of dusk had disappeared. I parked the car, walked to the glass front door, and gazed at my reflection in it—taking a moment before I turned the front door key she'd given me.

I'd been ashamed to look at my reflection for months—forgot I had one. I smiled at it before walking through the doorway.

I had been granted atonement for my "sins," and I was starting to feel at one with myself.

Perhaps that's why they call it "*at-one*-ment."

DAY **4**

VANISHING POINT

Dead in the water

On a frigid and crystal-clear night, the luxury cruise ship plowed through calm waters. The fur-wrapped passengers who ventured outside for a view enjoyed an unusually crisp peppering of stars in the night sky.

As midnight beckoned, the two veteran lookouts saw something. In the official report they would later describe it as "a dark mass that came through the haze;" nothing obviously visible until it was close, with "just a fringe at the top."

The lookouts immediately warned the bridge. The officer in charge took evasive measures.

He succeeded. But only in avoiding a head-on collision.

No more than sixty seconds later, the ship grazed alongside the "dark mass."

Two hours and forty minutes later, the ship was at the bottom of the Atlantic Ocean.

You know the name of the ship:

Titanic.

The mystery wasn't *why Titanic* sank or why it sank so fast—it grazed an iceberg in such a fashion that it sliced a 300-foot gash across five watertight compartments—a freak occurrence nobody would have planned for in her design.

The real mystery was why two of the most experienced lookouts in the White Star Line didn't *see* the iceberg earlier on a crystal-clear night, however fast the vessel was going. Even without binoculars (which weren't necessary on such a clear night and, using 1912 tech, could actually *impair* night vision and restrict peripheral awareness), the iceberg, 50-100 feet above the water and about 300 feet long, *should* have been visible.

The clue to solving the mystery was in the report regarding what the lookouts *said they saw*: "a dark mass that came through the haze... with just a fringe at the top."

That's a funny way to describe an iceberg. Perhaps we should focus on the key word in the report: *haze.*

So, what was that "haze?"

In principle, it was the same haze that sinks most people's *lives* without them knowing.

A mental haze.

Most people are lost in a false narrative. But one we wholeheartedly believe in.

On Day One we talked about the low point of our life story—the end of our "second act." Most people don't walk out of their own movie at the low point. They do something much worse: *they keep rewinding it and watching it over and over.*

And over.

There's a point where what happened to you stops being an event and starts being *who you are.*

Your "scar-script" becomes your introduction, your alibi, your explanation for everything you've done and *everything you haven't.*

You tell the story again and again. Sometimes to others. Sometimes just to yourself. The words change, the details shift, but the *shape* stays the same. It's the shape you've built your entire life around.

Death, divorce, loss, betrayal, trauma, these are all real things. What's *not* real is the false identity we build around them.

At first, it was a way to survive. The story gave meaning to the chaos. It gave you something solid to hold when the ground fell away. But over time, the story stopped being a tool *and became a cage.*

Two important clarifications:

1. **This is not the same thing as the Deleted Scene.** The Deleted Scene hides in the subconscious, but the scar-script plays out in full awareness—a deliberate performance we know we're giving. We're *conscious* of it.

2. **This should *not* be confused with PTSD** (Post Traumatic Stress Disorder). Crucial distinction: PTSD is a clinical reaction to trauma; I'm talking about an identity built around it. One is about what happened to you—the other is about who you believe you became because of it.

How to know if you're caught up in this all-too-common trap:

- If someone interrupts your scar-script, you feel an urge to defend it.

- If someone suggests you can move on, you feel like they're attacking you.

- If someone offers a different version of events, you feel rage. Not because it's untrue, but because it threatens the version of *you* that lives inside the story.

Why do we do it to ourselves?

For some reason, a phrase from a 1930s play went viral around 2016: "gaslighting." It stuck, and the herd ran with it. "He's gaslighting me... she gaslit me... stop gaslighting your dog, yada, yada." But the irony is this:

The biggest "gas lighter" you'll ever face is yourself.

The human mind is a story-making engine. It constantly rewrites memory, perception, and meaning to maintain a sense of coherence —*even when that coherence is false.*

When the truth threatens the psyche's stability, the mind doesn't say "I'm lying to myself." It says things like:

"That didn't really happen. *This* is what happened."

"It wasn't that bad."

"I was right to do that."

This is *self-gaslighting.*

When you have this condition, moving forward doesn't just feel hard, it feels dangerous. Because if you stop telling the scar-script, if you stop being the person who lived through that, then who are you?

People don't consciously quit in this situation; they drift.

And drifting is worse than quitting.

It means *you don't know* you're headed for a crash until it jumps up and bites you in the ass.

It's tunnel vision. It's an obsession. It's a comfort blanket. It's a distraction. It's a breeding ground for bias. It's a dystopia disguised as utopia. It's a written invitation to trouble.

It's a lie.

Regardless, most people cling to their scar-script as if it's a life raft. Why? Because they're unconsciously asking themselves this question:

"If I let go, will there be anything left of me?"

Worse, many people believe that awareness of their scar-script means they're awake.

This isn't "awake." It just means you're hurt with a story. It's an anchor disguised as a map.

But people mistakenly believe this endless processing will eventually guide them to where they need to be.

And to be fair, nobody to my knowledge has provided a lifeboat sturdy enough to give people an alternative that's preferable to their beloved but doomed scar-script. My aim is to provide you with that alternative before the end of this book. And it's not just a lifeboat. *It's the coast guard.*

But we first have to be *willing* to fire the signal flare. That's to say:

We have to make mental room for it first. And that means destroying all the illusions we have about ourselves and our lives.

We have to admit to and submit to, reality.

And if you can make it out of this maze of mirrors, you will have accomplished something most people never will.

So, before we discover what sank *Titanic*, let's ask what's slowly sinking *you*.

I stabbed at a leftover Yorkshire pudding. It deflated. I'd lost my appetite. My stomach was already full—with the knot I couldn't untie.

I'd begun the day flicking through the photo album. An angry sixteen-year-old glaring at me from the page as school report cards from the 1980s fell onto the floor—every grade a D or an E apart from history and English literature which were both As, with footnote comments from the homeroom teacher to the effect of "What the fuck?!" Lovely.

Then I'd headed out to Canterbury—in my rented car that boasted a rearview mirror—timing the drive to miss the notoriously bad traffic on the M25 motorway; the "road to nowhere" that circled greater London like a noose.

I was in Canterbury to liquidate a property and because my mother thought I should "see someone" in light of recent events. I had lived in that town previously and had befriended a therapist there, so I figured I'd "see someone" who was familiar with my scar-script—cheaper than starting from scratch.

I slouched against the bar in a pub, killing time before my appointment, swilling a half-full glass of ale after nibbling at a roast beef lunch.

I stared into my open laptop. My new book was coming along. I'd already written the first line:

Fuck.

Looking good, Jimbo.

I slammed the laptop shut in disgust. Restrained myself from throwing it at the wall.

I felt it.

Like a gravitational force pulling me down. I was teetering on the edge of that seductive and slippery slope into victimhood, seething thoughts compressing my chest:

Someone should pay...

Screw this...

I'll never bounce back from this...

I did all I could, played it right, and the world screwed me over...

... so now I'm just not going to give a crap. Do my time until it's over...

It wasn't my fault...

Why did this happen to ME...?

That last thought snapped me out of the pity-party. I loosened my grip on the glass after being close to crushing it into fragments.

Enough with the circle-talk.

And in that moment, one reason why I'd drifted off course and stopped believing became clearer: I grew frustrated with hearing the looping narratives of people who didn't seem to want to break free of them.

Don't get me wrong, I have many testimonials from people I genuinely helped simply by listening. But I wanted to fix them, and they wouldn't do their part.

They didn't want to heal. They just wanted to decorate the wreckage.

Now it all felt like a big lie.

"Wake up! Wake up! Snap out of it!"

That's what I *really* wanted to say to them, shaking them by the shoulders, as they relayed their scar-script for the *third time*, and not showing any desire to break free of it. Some people would continue to come to my live events year after year, God love them, but they came back with the same scar-script. I mean, great if they just wanted to hang out with me (and admittedly, some did), but they simply weren't listening and/or making any effort.

But now I was in their shoes, I could see it's much easier said than done.

Since my own crisis, I had been acting out *my* scar-script—trying to live a life that no longer existed—like the guy who loses his job but still gets on the train to work every morning so he can pretend it hadn't happened.

An initial period of recovery is indeed needed. But I'd had that time—ruminating over replays—and I knew it. It was time to practice what I had preached for so long.

But how?

I inhaled sharply and slapped a twenty-pound note on the bar. I needed some air. I grabbed the leather document pouch with all my old training notes, burst out of the pub, into swirling wind under a deathly gray sky, and found myself in a small square that framed a stone memorial cross, opposite the entrance to Canterbury cathedral.

The cathedral's ornate gateway drew me in, and a minute later I was inside. The somber air was heavy with history, that musky smell, the tombs. And the stories...

For as long as people have spoken, they have told stories. Stories explain the past, give meaning to suffering, and tell us who we are.

But stories also trap us if we aren't mindful; if we identify with them, if we get lost in them.

Geoffrey Chaucer saw this as far back as the 14th century. That's why his classic work *The Canterbury Tales* still matters. They aren't just old stories about people on a pilgrimage, headed for Canterbury cathedral. They are maps of human weakness. And one of them exposes the trap of the scar-script so clearly it's impossible to ignore: *The Wife of Bath's Tale:*

The Wife of Bath constantly refers to her five marriages and past experiences to justify her current views and actions. While initially this seems like confidence, she's actually trapped by these memories and uses them to create a defensive narrative.

Rather than living in the present, she's constantly recycling and reinterpreting her past to win arguments and gain social currency.

Sound like anyone you know?

Chaucer wasn't the first to expose this trap—he was just holding up a mirror to something already centuries old. Long before his pilgrims walked to Canterbury, crusaders marched to Jerusalem (often using Canterbury as a rest stop and blessing on the way).

They too believed they were on a sacred mission—chasing justice, purpose, and divine meaning. But many who survived found no salvation, only blood and ruin. And the deeper they went, the more that story consumed them.

That's the danger of scar-script addiction:

The longer you follow its path, the harder it is to admit it was leading nowhere. You have to either drop the story *or die living inside it.*

Behavioral economics calls it "the sunk cost fallacy." For our purposes, the sunk cost fallacy is the trap of staying in a scar-script just because you've already bled for it.

In every cathedral, the air hums with sarcophagi—monuments to people who once moved, spoke, fought, and then froze in their final pose. Most of us do the same long before we die.

Gazing at the tomb of The Black Prince—his gilded effigy lying in armor, hands clasped in prayer—I was reminded of a crusade of my own...

London Borough of Hammersmith, 1986. At age sixteen, the strict all-boys school I attended had become a powder keg under oppressive authority and ingrained tradition.

Every morning, we were barely through the gates of this Gothic castle before the same, cranky teacher, Mr. Stone, would bark at us for something. "Sheridan, wipe the eyeliner off!" (It was a 1980s thing).

On that particular morning, I vividly recall listening to Depeche Mode as I walked through the school gates when I heard Mr. Stone's voice competing with the lead singer's: "Sheridan, take that Walkman off!"

Interrupting my daily listening of the *Black Celebration* album was sacrilege.

I stopped and turned towards him, then stared at him before removing my headphones. A plastic eye patch beneath his spectacles covered his right eye, and an impatient exhale from his nostrils into the frigid air looked like dragon's breath.

We fantasized about that man's murder, and what it would mean to the pupil population: he'd become our very own Archduke Ferdinand assassination—a potential catalyst that might trigger chaos (We were studying 20th century political history, after all).

As I glared into a restroom mirror to reapply my war paint, I asked myself: *why just dream it?*

A stagnant waiting line for the dining hall sparked our insurrection. Occupying a square outside the hall, at least a hundred teenage schoolboys were hungry for their daily bread.

I decided to exploit this discontent of the masses to seize power, and the time was right to get our demands met (though I wasn't sure what our demands were other than mayhem). Like all revolutions, it would be triggered by terrorism, so if I were to become their leader I would need to engineer an act of terror.

I yelled at the boys in the lunch queue, "You're a bunch of fucking slaves!" and similar, inciting them to start surging the waiting line, like knights besieging a castle with a battering ram. And they complied with passion.

There wasn't just strength in numbers, there was *anonymity*, a tactic that would soon define the radical faction of our movement. Mr. Stone, the tyrant teacher, was the lunch monitor that day, and he was forced to let us in despite his yelling, red face.

It had begun.

But a more significant act of violence would be needed—it was time for that assassination. So, once we were all seated inside with our food and Mr. Stone's back was turned, from at least twenty-five yards, I launched a roasted potato at his head.

It was a Hail-Mary shot but it was a direct hit, and everyone saw it.

The audacity and accuracy of it was surreal, even for me.

A gravy-stained Mr. Stone yanked me by the ear, out of the masses to see Mr. Isaacs, the headmaster. But my subsequent "crucifixion"— through six lashes of a cane rod across my bare ass—only made me a martyr. And the legend of class U5R of '86 was set in motion. We even declared our own anthem: *Sledgehammer* by Peter Gabriel.

We shut down their sterile school library and its contrived collection of books through coordinated attacks on the silence with "noise bombs." A noise bomb was multiple, independently-operated cells of boys yelling gibberish at different times in different locations and then dispersing, innocently blending into bookshelves.

The librarians had no weapon against us other than a frantic *sshhhh!* hissed at nobody in particular. I watched my terrorist cells in action from the first-floor balcony, nodding my head in approval (and thus remaining "innocent" and untouchable). And, after this played out a few times in one afternoon, the staff closed the library in disgust.

Chemistry lessons were our best chance of burning the place down and believe me, we tried. Methane gas taps with no tube attached were "accidentally" opened and ignited to create flamethrowers, sulphuric acid got knocked over onto textbooks (whoops!), and inverted glass Petri dishes exploded like bombs when placed under the stool leg of any of our dissenters once they sat back down on it.

And the genius was that nobody was to blame. "*Another* bin fire, Sheridan? Well... everybody out! *Again!*"

"For the first time in the school's history," the headmaster hissed at one morning assembly, "the cafeteria was closed down because of the dinner ladies being bombarded with debris!" It was a proud accolade for our orchestrated riot against their lousy food. With special thanks to our catapult "archers" who covertly operated behind a wall of innocent faces.

Bullying of the weak or different became a thing of the past because we were all working together now, comrades against a common evil. The brainy kids gathered intel and let the other kids copy their homework. The small kids snuck into inaccessible spaces to plant devices and seize supplies. Pakistani kids taught everyone tactical vocabulary in Urdu for encoded communications ("Hamla Karo!" = Attack!). And rugby players ensured compliance and broke shit.

But as our cause had grown more radical, I could sense support from my comrades waning. I was informed about murmurings from some boys who were planning to "bump into" certain teachers at the train station. So I wondered if I'd been betrayed on that mid-march afternoon, after an English literature class on Shakespeare's *Julius Caesar*.

After class, I was sat down in front of my English literature teacher, Mr. Watts, for a private, one-on-one "chat." He no doubt suspected it was me who had cried "Havoc!" to let slip my dogs of war, but this parlay was going nowhere, I told myself.

Mr. Watts leaned against his desk, arms folded, glaring at me without saying a word. I sat at my desk and mirrored him, arms folded and glaring back.

Mr. Watts broke the silence with a single word: "Why?"

Trust an English literature teacher to search for the hidden meaning. But his question sent something hot and unwelcome bubbling up from my gut and into my head as I unconsciously attempted to answer his question...

90

Under a furrowed brow, my bitter glare jerked into a pitiful stare, and then I broke down into an uncontrollable torrent of tears.

Mr. Watts's angry demeanor melted away as he hurried towards me.

"What's wrong?" he said.

I howled at the ceiling tiles, blinded by tears, "My parents are getting divorced! My Dad is leaving us for another woman!" (This wasn't as common back then and I was the only kid in the class harboring this shameful secret.) I sobbed against the desk, harder than before.

To my surprise, the oppressor's envoy—Mr. Watts—threw his arms around my shoulders and told me it would be okay, and that he was there for me if I ever needed anything.

I could no longer try to destroy people like Mr. Watts, so I ordered my brave comrades to lay down their arms. A single word from the enemy quashed The Rebellion of '86, like a tranquilizer dart fired at my raging soul.

Alternate endings

"Every revolution devours its children." —Mr. Watts

You might not be flinging potatoes at your antagonist, but you're in a similar war.

When you're invested in a scar-script, abandoning it feels like abandoning an entire functioning world you spent a lifetime building.

That's not easy.

But it's necessary.

The scar-script starts to collapse the moment it's questioned. It's like realizing you're in a dream, and the whole thing begins to glitch and collapse.

So what about you?

What cause are *you* fighting for that's a cover for something you don't want to *feel?*

People could walk out of the "haze" anytime.

But most don't.

Why?

Often because they're still chasing "closure" and "validation" —*from a story that never wanted to give them either.*

Closure and validation. Let's talk about these widely accepted ideas that are thought to be a mandatory part of healing, necessary before someone can move on with their life.

Let me start by re-emphasizing something I said earlier:

I'm *not* saying trauma isn't real or that it doesn't require an *initial* period of processing.

This isn't about painting on a "stiff upper lip" or to just "keep calm and carry on" (even if I am British).

Everyone needs comfort *at the time* of crisis, but you're past that point or you wouldn't have picked up a book subtitled *"Seven Days to Reforge Your Life."*

What I *am* talking about are the dangers of staring at the abyss for too long and falling for the trap of scar-script addiction long *after* the crisis.

So, what about "closure?"

Let's use my 1986 schoolboy story as the example. I was the antagonist in poor Mr. Watts's story. To be clear, when he asked me that single word question—Why?–he wasn't seeking "closure." He just wanted the mayhem to stop.

As it happened though, we could say Mr. Watts got "closure" by understanding my situation, comforting me, and elegantly turning an enemy into an ally in one fell swoop. He even got an ipso facto apology from the teenage hellraiser, case closed.

That's the kind of "closure" people want and wait for. To understand the antagonist and then get them to see their wicked ways before conceding.

To quote another tired self-help platitude (and it's not wrong), "Hurt people hurt people." Great. And now the story ends, with us all becoming better people for the experience as we hold hands in a chain, walking into the sunset together, all singing "Kumbaya..."

But that's not how real life usually goes, is it?

Let's consider an alternate ending to the 1986 story...

Mr. Watts broke the silence with a single word: "Why?"

How pathetic! I homed in on his weakness as a shark reacts to blood in the water.

"Fuck you!" I said, cackling into his face. Then I spat on the ground before him.

"Right," he yelled. "Go to see the headmaster, at once!"

I shrugged as I lunged up from my desk. "Sure," I said. "I'll tell that crusty old wanker to go fuck himself, too. Maybe I'll thrash his bald head with that cane of his while I'm at it!"

I couldn't wait to tell my comrades about *this* one.

Where's your "closure" now?

Perhaps your need for closure then descends into a thirst for revenge. Perhaps *that* will give you closure...

Except, it won't. At best, it will throw you off course. At worst, it will "devour" you...

Listen:

Some people simply want to watch the world burn *for no reason.*

And you just happened to cross their path as they were lighting the match.

Seeking vengeance against such a person will only burn you up, too.

Maybe you'll comfort yourself with the idea of "karma." If it helps you move on, great. Use it. But don't count on it, don't get distracted as a spectator of it, and *don't delay your life waiting for it to show.*

If you *really* believe in karma, then trust it. Let go. Move forward and let the Universe do its job.

And if you *don't* believe in karma? Then what are you doing? If it's all random chaos—no cosmic repayment plan—what control do you think you have? And what's the point of clinging to "closure" from a story that has no author, no justice, and no resolution?

Regarding those who wrong us, I try to remember three things:

1. People are their own punishment.

2. You're not forgiving them for their benefit; you're forgiving them for *your* benefit.

3. Other people's opinion of me is none of my business.

As Epictetus said, "If someone tried to take control of your body and make you a slave, you would fight for freedom. Yet how easily you hand over your mind to anyone who insults you. When you dwell on their words and let them dominate your thoughts you make them your master."

Whether you want "closure" from someone who wronged you or not (perhaps it was a natural death, etc.) isn't the point.

The point is this:

The need for "closure" usually makes a third party the gatekeeper of your evolution.

And that is unacceptable.

We can choose closure any time we wish.

Next axiom in the crosshairs: validation.

Of course, we all want to feel seen and heard, but I'm referring to the kind of validation we think we need in order for our pain to heal.

Let's say I wave a magic wand and declare: "Your feelings about that terrible incident are officially validated."

Now what?

Does anything actually shift? Are you suddenly free, unburdened, walking forward?

No. Because validation isn't healing.

It's approval. A nod from the outside world that says your pain is "real enough" to count. But here's the trap:

If someone else needs to confirm your experience before you're allowed to move on, then they control your release. You've made them the judge of your reality.

Now you're waiting on a stamp of approval that may never come.

Validation is just another stalling tactic— emotional bureaucracy. A way to stay hurt but be applauded for it.

But what happens when the applause doesn't come?

What if the people you hoped would understand you... don't?

Worse, what if they blame you?

What then?

Do you pause your life? Fold your arms and wait for someone to say, "Yes, you really did suffer"?

Validation is a leash. And you're holding your own collar, waiting for someone else to unclip it.

Again, and to put it another way: validation is necessary at impact. But clinging to it during recovery is like asking the paramedic to hold your hand five years after the crash.

Here's another alternate ending to the story:

Mr. Watts broke the silence with a single word: "Why?"

I sniffed. "Just stuff at home."

He nodded, gave me a soft smile, and said, "That must be tough. I see you. You're doing your best."

Then he let me go.

And I left the room with my ego fed, my story intact... *and nothing changed.*

No shift. No release. Just more justification for staying angry. **Validation didn't liberate me. It licensed the war to go on.**

When Mr. Watts reached out to comfort me—after I broke down in front of him—it wasn't validation I was given. He didn't say, "You're right. You're justified. Poor you." He didn't stamp my story with approval.

What he gave me was *presence.* A human moment. That was enough. That's the initial "hug" we all need *at the time of the crisis.*

He didn't validate my war—he disarmed it. He didn't applaud my pain—he simply didn't run from it.

And here's the point:

That moment helped me shift because I wasn't trying to be seen; I was finally just being real.

No performance. No applause. Just *truth.* And that's what broke the loop.

Validation is *performed pain.* Truth is *what heals.*

Because truth doesn't need permission from anyone or anything.

Painting yourself into a corner

Is there any deeper insight about why humans are so partial to scar-scripts or any looping narrative, even though they are doing so *consciously* and are *conscious* of the fact it's blocking their growth?

The answer was in the question: "consciously" and "conscious."

As touched on in Day Two, consciousness is what separates humans from the other animals, but what is it, actually?

Let's figure that out by comparing humans to other animals and the common things we assume consciousness gives us that make humans so different from them:

Tool use? Nope...
Some octopuses carry coconut shells for armor.
Crows shape twigs into hooks.

Learning and problem-solving? Nope...
Elephants stack cubes to reach fruit.
Rats escape mazes faster than most humans escape bad marriages.

Communication? Nope...
Bees dance the coordinates to food.
Dolphins name each other with whistles.

Self-awareness? Nope...
Magpies recognize themselves in mirrors.

So how can we say that consciousness makes us different from other animals? What is consciousness doing for us that it's not doing for them?

This:

Dolphins don't hold a grudge about the shark that bit them.
They don't swim in circles rehearsing how it made them feel unlovable.

Crows don't ask for closure from the cat that ate their cousin.
They just dive-bomb the bastard and get on with their day.

Elephants don't spend years journaling about the poacher's betrayal.
They just remember the face and flatten the village.

Octopuses don't spiral into an identity crisis because they used the wrong shell.
They change color, squirt ink, and leave.

(Sidebar: Even the most intelligent creatures—the elephants who remember, the whales who retaliate—remain on the near side of the threshold. They feel grief, anger, and memory, but they do not step outside those feelings to narrate them. They can't remember that they remember, like we can. They do not say, *"I am the one who lost,"* or *"I will become my pain."* Their consciousness is immediate, not recursive. They live inside experience; we live inside our retelling of it. Elephants and whales feel everything—but they don't turn their feelings into myths, religions, or neuroses. Humans do.)

Animals experience. *Humans narrate.*

Animals don't need closure. They need survival, and therefore they need to eliminate threats. We survive. And then we build a prison out of memory and call it "healing."

"But I am not an animal!" I hear you cry.

Tell that to your nervous system the next time it's flooded with cortisol. Tell it to your limbic system when it hijacks your logic because someone looked at you funny. You are absolutely an animal. But okay...

You're right. You're not *just* an animal. You're an animal with a special *type* of consciousness I will refer to as:

Subjective consciousness.

You have a mind that can watch itself suffer and then tell a story about why it deserves to. That's what makes you "special." Not because you're more evolved. But because you're more *trapped...*

Unmastered, *subjective* consciousness creates the ability to watch yourself suffer, and then turn it into a brand.

Here's another way of looking at it:

Bowl of fruit = reality

*A **painting** of that bowl of fruit = subjective consciousness*

And there's the rub...

Because paintings, like subjective consciousness, are, well, *subjective.* In other words, **the bowl of fruit and the painting of it are not the same thing, right?**

It's when *subjective* consciousness snatches the paintbrush that things can go wrong.

How that bowl of fruit is *portrayed* depends on the *story* the artist wants to tell. This story is shaped by the artist's *experience*.

If Vermeer ("Girl with a Pearl Earring," et al) painted the bowl of fruit, it would be uncannily true to reality.

If Picasso painted the bowl of fruit, it would feature an apple having an existential crisis, a banana screaming into a void, and a grape with three noses wondering why its mother left.

If Jackson Pollock (the artist behind those paint-splash parties) painted the bowl of fruit, it would look like the fruit had a panic attack in zero gravity and exploded across the canvas.

So the big question is this:

Are you Vermeer or Picasso?

Or, if you have really serious issues—like that unruly schoolboy in 1986— are you Jackson Pollock on a bad day?

It's your choice, but if we are to grow as individuals we need to break free of the addiction to looping scar-scripts.

And that means we must "paint" our perceptions of reality as close as possible to how Vermeer would: with brutal clarity.

Because every perspective—like every painting—has a hidden force shaping it. A focal point the whole image bends around.

In art, it's called a "vanishing point."

In life, it's often your pain.

So if your "vanishing point" is warped—if it's based on grief, blame, or the need to be seen—then *what you perceive will begin to lie to you.*

Everything around it will shift to fit the distortion.

And the more focused on it you are, the less you'll see what's really coming.

That's not healing. That's hallucination.

Chasing your tale

"None are more hopelessly enslaved than those
who falsely believe they are free."
—Goethe.

Disillusionment makes us sad and angry. And I wager that the world has never been so full of disillusioned people as now, because the illusion has never been so prevalent and propagated.

But one cannot experience disillusionment without harboring an illusion in the first place.

Illusion = eventual disillusion = tragedy

So we are immune to disillusionment when we have no illusions.

That doesn't mean cynicism or negativity. It simply means reality.

The hardest truth isn't letting go of the past, it's letting go of who you *think* it made you. That's your "painting" of reality:

Trauma = reality
*Your **painting** of the trauma = ?*

Let's put our gift of consciousness to work for good for a change. This gift allows us to imagine things and visualize, so imagine this:

Your journey is a long tunnel. Ten feet wide, by ten feet tall. Cold stone walls.

You're walking down this tunnel. Endless repetition. You can see as far as your sight allows, and on the horizon you see where the walls and ceiling of the tunnel converge.

There is light at this point of convergence on the horizon.

You walk and walk, getting closer and closer to that light. It seems like you're making progress. You can hear people cheering you on.

As you get closer, though, something seems off...

That point of convergence is getting bigger, closer. The tunnel isn't opening up.

That's when you hit a wall. It was an illusion.

Not light. Not freedom. Just... canvas.

You inspect this painting.

It's disgusting.

Acrylic over oil over charcoal over dried tears. Flakes of it peeling off in clumps. Underneath, older layers. Hand-me-down trauma. The "I'm not enough" basecoat no one ever stripped away.

Each layer a loop. Each brush stroke a lie. Each revision an attempt to justify why you're still here, still stuck, still not free.

It's flaking, peeling, rancid with old meaning.

Every session. Every quote. Every person who hurt you. Every breakthrough you posted about but never lived. All there.

This isn't healing.

This is hoarding.

A shrine to everything you were supposed to let go of.

And it's blocking your path.

Now, I just placed a match in one of your hands and a matchbox in the other.

Take one last look at that painting. All that paint, it's practically begging to be burned.

Now light that match and burn it!

Burn through the narrative.

Watch the canvas ignite.

Make sure the flame burns through every comforting scene you painted—the heroic trauma, the deserving victim, the long-awaited redemption.

Done.

Tattered and smoldering, the shredded canvas swings in the breeze.

What's on the other side of it?

Uncertainty. Freedom. Your future. Adventure.

Reality.

Raw, unfiltered, unscripted.

Now run through it!

Run through what's left of that crap...

... like a Dallas Cowboys cheerleader...

... brandishing matches instead of pompoms.

And don't look back—you're not going that way.

Step off

In mythology, Oedipus defeated the Sphinx, but in doing so he defeated himself—because he interpreted reality through a protective story. His prophecy was the wound—an event he thought too unbearable to face—so he built his whole identity around escaping it.

Every decision he made was a defense, a story meant to outsmart pain. Yet that story became his trap. The more he tried to control the narrative, the deeper he sank into it.

The same blindness to reality sank the *Titanic*...

The iceberg had already hit. The loss was real.

But hitting the iceberg wasn't the death sentence; it was the failure to act decisively after impact.

We don't drown when life sinks our ship. We drown when we wait too long to swim.

If we're not awake and living in reality, we're going to keep bumping into "icebergs" that seem to just come out of the haze and sink our lives.

Even the *Titanic* had a vanishing point. On that crystal-clear night, the lookouts weren't blind, they were focused. *But they were focused on the wrong thing.* They were focused on something *that wasn't real.*

Reports later revealed that a false horizon had formed; an optical illusion caused by temperature inversion and haze forming a "cold water mirage." It distorted the line where sea met sky. The iceberg was there, but the lookouts' visual perspective had bent around a vanishing point that wasn't based on reality.

That's what happens when your vanishing point is built on false perception. The story you believe becomes the iceberg, you don't.

And the iceberg won't care how well you understood your pain.

Cathedrals or concentration camps? Humans are evidently capable of building both. Not just in the physical world, but inside our minds, too, I thought to myself.

I realized this was my fork in the road. As I took one last panoramic gaze around Canterbury cathedral, my eyes met the stained-glass Redemption Window: Noah releasing a dove from the Ark after the flood, Jesus emerging from a tomb.

Ultimately, nobody but me could make me better. Our darkest hour is only an hour of our lives. Anything longer than that is our own doing.

The past is to learn from, not lean on.

I didn't need to "see someone" about my scar-script, I simply needed to burn it. The only remaining reason I had to rummage through the ashes was to find my phoenix and ride it the hell out of here.

I cancelled the therapy session as I turned and headed for the exit. I needed to head home. To escape the M25 traffic.

To breathe.

And to make a confession to everyone who cared about me:

I hadn't attempted suicide back in Florida. I'd merely fallen asleep while I was cleaning the gun. That empty bottle of vodka? It's where I kept the cleaning fluid. Yes, I was at rock-bottom—the low-point of my entire life. But the only suicide I wanted now was metaphysical— to incinerate my old life. Jenna and my mother had filled in the blanks with their own minds, and I didn't correct them because it had fed my scar-script.

But now my scar-script was ash. Discarding it left me feeling adrift, but also full of potential...

A blank canvas to paint on.

A Vermeer.

Never again would I pander to people's self-pity. I would instead work on nurturing people's latent strength. I would no longer ride the bandwagon of the mainstream healing-industrial complex. I would build something better. Something honest. And if people didn't want it at least I'd sleep at night.

I yanked all my old training notes from the leather document pouch and threw them in the trash on the way out of the cathedral.

Are you coming?

Or shall I leave you here among the tombs?

DAY **5**

GAME ON

Mobilizing memory

Confidence. Where did it go?

Nowhere.

Confidence isn't learned or won or built, or any other story that begins with *lack*.

It's remembered.

Remembered from the high points. Remembered from how you broke out of the low points.

You were *born* confident. And then life tried to beat it out of you.

But we can't *remember* confidence while we're hypnotized by the illusions of the Deleted Scene and the Vanishing Point. Illusions that buried who we are and all we are meant to become.

So we burned them.

But if you have nothing to replace them with, you're no better than the things you burned. Destruction leaves a vacuum. So here is the next issue facing us:

Nature abhors a vacuum, and *fear adores a vacuum*.

Lose something and hesitate, and fear will rush in with ten false futures. So we must move *now*, before fear colonizes the crater.

Move where?

How?

Slow down. And know this:

The antidote to fear is commitment.

Not courage. Courage waits for clarity, and fear loves that. What kills fear stone-dead is commitment.

Cold-blooded. Final.

A *non-retractable decision*. Once the decision is made, *fear becomes noise*, not obstruction.

The antidote to fear—commitment—is to swear an oath: *"This is the hill I die on."*

Do or die.

Whether you're crawling from the wreckage of a broken relationship, financial ruin, or spiritual collapse, it doesn't matter. The battlefield is different, but the law is the same.

What you *personally* fight for—the cause etched into your DNA—will hopefully be revealed in high-definition before the end of the book. For now, you don't need a *reason* to fight...

You just need to refuse to rot where you fell.

And that's what I *demand* of us now.

The will to stand, to hit back, to not back down *must* exist *before* the vision for your life is cast.

Because otherwise, when adversity shows up along the way—and it will—you won't follow through. You'll say it wasn't meant to be. But that's just your old fear pretending to be destiny.

It probably *was* meant to be...

You just didn't know how to take a punch.

So right now, this isn't about direction.

It's about defiance in the face of adversity.

And it's about outright rejection of the common knee-jerk goal we default to immediately after loss: to get back what we had or to run to "Plan B" with our tail between our legs. That reflex is born of lack, fear, and desperation. And whatever we want from that place, life gives us the opposite.

I don't want you to reclaim what you once had. I want you to claim all you are truly meant to be.

Your current situation is not a setback. It's leverage. In *The Art of War*, Sun Tzu wrote: "Throw your soldiers into positions whence there is no escape, and they will prefer death to flight. If they will face death, there is nothing they may not achieve."

He went on (parentheses mine): "When you surround an army, leave an outlet (for them)."

Sun Tzu knew both sides of this law. When it's your army, no escape sharpens their resolve. But when it's your enemy, the same condition makes them lethal.

Why? Because when there's no retreat, something ancient activates: The will to *win or die trying*.

When people's backs are against the wall they become dangerous.

Nothing to lose, everything to play for.

And that's us.

That's harnessing the *power* of rock-bottom.

Take the shot

I was easing into a tranquil life in rural England. And that feeling you get when you're on vacation seeped in: Maybe I just won't go back.

Perhaps I could scrape by for several years until my airline pension kicked in, do some freelance work. Fly back to America when I felt like it, see my kids, stay connected. Maybe meet someone—try marriage again and pretend the third time isn't surrender.

I hadn't gotten up yet. But when I did, I'd look at property listings in Bath—a town I'd always felt attracted to and wasn't far from my mother and sister. I lay in bed, sipping tea as birdsong outside my window embraced a sunny morning.

I flicked through the photo album. A confident 18-year-old version of me—a hockey player—posed for the camera like he owned the future.

He looked immortal. Unstoppable.

What the hell happened to him?

Thank God for ice hockey. Or I'd probably have ended up in juvenile hall...

Hockey became my world. After my parents divorced my teenage aggression was vented on the ice, playing in Britain's premier league for Richmond Flyers (a district of South West London—the same Richmond of *Ted Lasso* TV show fame). By 1988, at just 18 years old, I'd made it to the first line-up, to the disgust of the veteran I'd replaced.

I was the upstart rookie, prematurely drafted in from the junior team in the 1986/7 season. And I was hiding something from my fellow warriors in this new tribe:

I was afraid of fighting.

I could outskate half the team. I could score goals. I could handle the insults and opposing players sneakily spearing me in the ribs with their sticks. Shielded by body armor, I could handle a 250-pound giant ramming me into the boards at 25 mph. I could handle a puck (a.k.a. rubber bullet) launched toward my visor at 100 mph.

But the thought of getting into a fist fight terrified me...

... in the only team sport in the world that tolerates fighting as part of the game, in a sport where the paying crowd—especially at this level—*demands* fist fights.

We trained hard into the wee hours of the morning, including punishing endurance drills until some players puked. Red line, blue line, red line. The Canadian coach—an NHL veteran—was tough as nails and took no prisoners.

At least there were no fights in practice.

But on game day?

When those swirling spotlights glared onto fresh ice to the blaring soundtrack of *Welcome to the Jungle* by Guns N' Roses? When we skated through the steam and sweat, and into the crowd's war-cries...?

That's when I was reminded this wasn't a game. And this wasn't an ice arena. Not to the crowd. It was an amphitheater. And we were the gladiators.

And eventually, like all fears that aren't faced, mine found me.

We were playing a home game against Telford Tigers; a team notorious for intimidation tactics, cheap shots... and fist fights.

In the closing minutes of the third period in a brutal, tied game, seconds *after* I shot the puck, one of their giant players rammed into me at full speed, sending me flying across the ice.

An illegal move. No big deal. I was fine, and the giant had just given us a power play for that pointless cheap shot. The referee blew his whistle and skated towards the giant with both arms raised to call the penalty. I got back up.

Then the giant threw his gauntlets down, flipped his helmet off, and raised his fists, glaring at me hungrily...

The crowd roared.

Fuck.

The referees tried to block the giant, but he pushed them off, just staring at me, beckoning me, smiling confidently...

I froze.

My helmet stayed on. My gloves stayed on. My stick lowered.

I skated backwards a few feet.

The giant laughed before turning towards the penalty box.

Then it rained popcorn on me.

The crowd booed me.

The coach gave me the signal to get off the ice.

The other players ignored me on the bench. Not even a look. Not even a word.

I'd never felt so hated.

The team was my family. The fans were my fuel. It was all I had.

I didn't lose a fight. I lost the ground beneath me.

What if you DON'T?

When Nietzsche famously said, "What doesn't kill me makes me stronger" he probably didn't imagine we'd defang it with pastel fonts and turn it into a Hallmark-card. Nietzsche didn't mean "You survived, good job." When Nietzsche wrote that in *Twilight of the Idols*, he wasn't romanticizing pain...

He meant this:

Pain must be used as fuel, or it becomes decay.

We all have points in our past we wish we could return to—so we could act differently. We yearn for a time machine to take us into the past so we could change our present. If only, right?

But we *do* have a time machine...

With just one catch: it can only go into the future.

Step inside it. Ten years forward. No changes—trace the trajectory your life is on *now*. Only account for the plans *you actually have in motion now.*

What do you see? How does life look? The same? Worse?

Now get in that time machine and return to the present.

What would you tell yourself in present day? What you shouldn't do, sure. But what would you tell yourself to *do*?

Look that future unlived life in the eye.

And ask yourself now: "What if I *don't*?"

You think the pain of fighting is bad?

Try living with the version of yourself that backed down, chickened out, or who was afraid to even make an effort. Try looking at photos of who you used to be and wondering where the fire went, and when exactly you let it go out.

Listen...

Fighting spirit doesn't come from "positive thinking." It comes from realizing that *not* fighting will cost you *everything*.

Fear of failure isn't a problem. *It's the permission slip to make a commitment.*

Failure only breaks you when you accept it as final. The moment you entertain the notion you are beaten, then you are beaten.

Until that final buzzer sounds, failure is never final; it's *temporary*. It's not real until you decide it is. The moment you call it permanent—*that's when it kills you.*

Fear of pain if you *do* it?

Pain isn't the limit. Perception is. Most people don't act because it hurts. They act because *they have to*. And here's what no one's told you:

You can survive far more pain than you're currently choosing to avoid.

The system sells safety as virtue. To stay put and hunker down. To shrug and say, "I am enough." But guess what?

You're not here to be "enough." You're here to discover and fulfill your destiny. To step into what you were truly meant to become. You're here to be *all in*.

If you're not fully engaged with that?

Then, no. You are *not* "enough." Not yet.

What if I told you now that someone you loved would die unless you *did* it.

Made that call. Quit that job. Left that partner. Launched that idea...

You'd do it. Trembling or not.

Therefore, it's not a mental capacity issue.

It's an urgency issue.

So get urgent.

Ten years into the future may seem like a long way off. It may seem like plenty of time for "things to figure themselves out." But left in your blindside, it will be on you in no time. And now, thanks to your time machine, you know what it looks like...

So ask it. Scream it:

What if I don't!?

Because once you answer that? You'll never wait again.

Ignore fear of failure, and just take the shot. Maybe you win, maybe you lose, but either way you now have a pulse. And you are wiser for the failure, provided you learned from it.

Commitment is the explosive that blows up fear. And urgency is the fuse...

But then uncertainty stops us lighting it.

We want certainty: "Okay, if I commit to doing this, what are the chances I pull it off?" But that's not commitment. That's conditional loyalty to a possible outcome.

That's asking for guarantees in a world that only rewards resolve.

True commitment doesn't ask, "Will it work?" It declares, "I will make it work, or die trying."

Most people want odds. But commitment means oaths.

Uncertain future? I say: Good! *Let* it be uncertain...

An uncertain future is a *good thing*. It means we can shape it. It means today's limits don't define tomorrow's power.

Uncertainty means you're standing in pure potential.

Uncertainty can paralyze the hesitant. Or it can ignite the one who's ready and willing. When the path is unclear, that means *no one owns it yet.*

And that's our opportunity. If the future were certain, it would already belong to someone else. But because it's not, you can take it.

The future doesn't exist until someone commits to it. Make that person you.

People often conveniently confuse pragmatism with fear of uncertainty. Many times, it's not pragmatism; it's fear masquerading as wisdom.

Uncertainty makes waiting feel smart.

I used to have a client who was obsessed with getting his "ducks in a row." Every time we would discuss fighting spirit and getting down to business, he would bring up those ducks—which never seemed to all conveniently line up for him. Like so many of us, he got "stuck on the ducks." And I knew this was simply fear of uncertainty in disguise...

"Yes... I get you. I really do. I just need to get my ducks in a row, first," he would say.

Following week:

"So, did you get all your ducks in a row?" I asked.

"No."

"Why not?"

"There are more ducks now."

Just shoot the fucking ducks, already!

Okay, I didn't actually say that.

But it gave me an idea...

The way I eventually talked him out of his fear was by using a concept I call "Ready, fire, aim." It seemed apt as it aligned with his persistent dependency on a metaphor about that carnival game involving shooting metal ducks with a pellet gun. Here's how it works:

The expression is usually "Ready, aim, fire," right? As in you take aim before you pull the trigger. Makes sense... if life's targets stood still.

But the ducks in that game are moving, just like time, *just like our lives passing us by.*

If you've ever done any shooting, even in a carnival game, you may recall that your follow-up shot—the shot taken after your initial shot—is more accurate.

You may have missed that first shot, but *now you're in the game—* you're recalibrating—so next time you're not going to miss.

So, I say, "Ready, *fire,* aim." Take the shot. Then adjust.

And if the ducks are running all over the place, and they won't conveniently get in a neat little row for you?

Use a shotgun.

Just get in the game.

So, I politely made my client eat his own metaphor.

"Okay, I'll do it," he declared with tightened lips as he slapped his thigh. "But what's Plan B?"

Grrrr...

Classic. But it's a good question—just not in the way he intended it: What *is* "Plan B?"

When life knocks us on our ass, the tendency is to stay down and adopt a lower place in the pecking order. To trade dreams for dust. To settle for "Plan B."

Sure, it's sensible to have some emergency supplies, savings, and that sort of thing. But that's not a Plan B, that's just common sense. I'm talking about a *life plan.* Plan B is how most people *live,* and even if they don't realize it their soul does—as a small piece of it dies with every lost sunrise.

You've heard of a mission statement, right? Plan B is a *sub*-mission statement.

It's *sub*-mission; it's literally *beneath* your *true* mission: a new and noble mission you will begin defining before the end of this book. You know you're here for more. But Plan B keeps you playing small.

Plan B is not the unsung hero who saves you in your darkest hour; it's the unsung villain who makes it darker.

The only Plan B that's acceptable is to get back to Plan A.

Plan B can be an enticing exit ramp off the freeway to your true destiny, taken when you decide the drive is too much, or because "passengers" told you to, or because a situation *temporarily* demanded it. But if we're not careful, a rest stop becomes the *full stop* at the end of your story.

Time to re-enter the freeway and get where you were always meant to be.

Feed the underdog

I should've enjoyed touring properties in Bath. Fresh ground. But every viewing—no matter how nice it was—gave me a vague sinking feeling. Like I was running away. A new and nameless quest called out from far away.

I huffed. Time for a meal break. I had packed a "ploughman's lunch"; British for whatever scraps one finds lying around. But mine today was the typical variety: a hunk of hearth bread, a lump of Cheddar cheese (the real-deal, made in Cheddar, just twenty minutes away from my location), an apple, and the quintessential Branston pickle.

Earlier, I'd noticed a small castle perched high on a hill, watching over the town, but I had never visited it before. I decided to drive up there to eat lunch beneath it.

On the winding drive up that leafy hill, my incomplete recollection of the 1988 incident tailed me like a police car preparing to pull me over...

Richmond, 1988. Mid-week practice finished at 1 am—the only time we could train was after the public skating sessions. As the scent of perfume and popcorn faded, and the sounds of their flirting and frivolity switched into slapping pucks and pinging goalposts, that night I wished I could've been just like them: a happy spectator.

Practice was over. My legs were shot. I wanted a hot shower and to get home to my bed. But as I skated towards the exit gate, a familiar voice called out to me from behind:

"James! Stay for some extra practice, eh?" said one of our Canadian imports from the first offensive line. Every British premier league team was allowed up to three "imports:" usually NHL-level players from Canada or America. And, as I spun around, I was facing two of ours: one wearing a Toronto jersey, the other wearing a Calgary jersey.

"Sure," I said, putting my gloves back on. Fuck. Seriously?

Calgary jersey put his mouthguard back in, concealing the gap where his two front teeth used to be, and started circling me like a wolf flanking prey, then sprayed ice to stop behind me. Toronto jersey stayed put, casually leaning on his stick, looking me up and down.

"What do you want to practice... *eh?*" I said to Toronto, mimicking that Canadian habit of adding "eh?" to the end of sentences—an inside joke the three of us shared.

But tonight, they weren't laughing.

Calgary—behind me—shoved me hard, using his stick as a crossbar.

I spun around, confused.

Toronto skated at me.

"What's the..." I began.

Then the punch came.

They kept their gloves on as they battered my helmet instead of my face. But it still shocked me.

I froze.

Calgary punched the side of my helmet so hard I fell to the ground.

"Get up!" Toronto yelled.

"What's the matter, eh?" Calgary laughed. "*Useless!*"

Something snapped inside. They were no longer my brothers-in-arms. Not the ones I knew, joked with, drank with, and fed pucks to. I jumped to my feet and swung at Calgary's face. He easily dodged my fist, my unspent energy spinning me around like an off-balance figure skater.

So, while I was off-balance, Calgary effortlessly pushed me to the ground again with a single hand.

"That's not how you do it," Toronto said, shaking his head.

"*Get up!*" Calgary yelled, throwing his gauntlets down.

As I jumped to my feet again, Calgary grabbed me by the front of my jersey with one hand, his other hand cocked back and ready to punch, his back skate dug in like an icepick...

But no punch came.

"*That's* how you do it," Toronto said, pointing at Calgary's hands and skates. "Don't get all emotional...and lose your cool."

Calgary froze in position like a teaching aid as Toronto glided closer, his softly growling skates cutting the silence. "Watch closely..."

I clenched my jaw. "Okay. Show me."

Why do we cheer for underdogs?

We don't.

We cheer for underdogs who show their teeth.

It's not so much because underdogs winning means justice gets done, or because it makes things "fair."

Love it or hate it, Sylvester Stallone's *Rocky* franchise grossed in excess of $1.3 billion, making it perhaps the most iconic example of people loving the underdog story. Would *Rocky* have been nearly as commercially successful if it was all about fairness?

Of course not. He doesn't even win the fight in the first film! People cheered the war, not the win. We know what it's like not to be picked, not to be seen... *until we force them to see us.* Everyone wants to believe that if they give everything, if they *commit without fallback*, they can rise from nothing.

And what is the part of those films most people remember? The part that gives people goosebumps? The part where the score is most powerful?

Training.

Running up those steps.

Channeling anger, regret, fear—whatever we've been dealt—into focused energy.

We love underdogs because *they make a commitment. They swear an oath.* They don't succumb to shortcuts, cheap distractions, or dopamine traps. Because they're prepared to put all the sweaty work in while everyone else is sleeping (literally and figuratively), to do whatever it takes, whatever the sacrifice. And something else...

The underdog's secret weapon is *mastery*.

That's the hidden truth we all know but conveniently shy away from ... ironically, while simultaneously worshipping professional athletes—living examples of the cost and rewards of mastery.

But how can we possibly muster enough enthusiasm to make such a commitment about just one thing? Herein lies the core issue for everyone. And the operative word is "enthusiasm." You have it. You were born with it. You just forgot about it. And here, in this book, you will soon remember it—the thing you were built for.

But we must first clear the road for its homecoming. We must face the fear that wants to put up roadblocks for the parade.

Or *any* fear, for that matter.

The worst that could happen

"Cowards die many times before their deaths;
The valiant never taste of death but once..."
—Shakespeare's *Julius Caesar*,
Act II, Scene II.

What's the worst that could happen? In other words, what is our greatest fear?

That we could die.

But that's not the worst that *could* happen. It's the worst that *will* happen. Therefore, our greatest fear is of an inevitability. Julius Caesar continued:

"Of all the wonders that I yet have heard,
It seems to me most strange that men should fear;
Seeing that death, a necessary end,
Will come when it will come."

Death is the ultimate fear. If we can face that fear, we can face any fear, including our personal phobias and hang-ups.

So let's face our shared ultimate fear. Let's square up to death and look it in the eye.

The *Katha Upanishad*—one of the oldest and most beloved stories in Hinduism—is a story of a boy who did exactly that...

The boy—named Nachiketa—was brought before Yama, the god

of death. But instead of pleading for safety or escape, the boy asked Death to teach him the mystery of what comes after life.

But Yama didn't answer. Not right away. First, he tempted the boy—with wealth, long life, pleasure, beautiful women. Every distraction, every escape hatch.

Why?

Yama wasn't being cruel; he was cleaning the boy's lens. If Nachiketa had taken the gifts, it would have proved he wasn't ready to hear the answer.

But Nachiketa refused all the gifts. He didn't want comfort. He wanted the truth. Clever lad...

Because once you stop reaching for the false life, you become ready to face real death. And that's when you learn how to *live*.

Ask anyone who's had a near-death experience. Feel their energy. They don't waste time. They don't chase likes. They don't play for status. Something in them has been burned clean. And what remains is terrifying to most people, because it's pure. Those who faced death, looked over the edge and lived to tell it, they walk like every second matters. Because it does.

Immanuel Kant, the 18th-century German philosopher, didn't fear death. He dissected it. He believed true freedom could only exist when we stop using life as a means to avoid discomfort and start acting from principle. He wrote (paraphrased): "The idea of death, and the fear it excites, not only restrains many from vice, but spurs others on to virtue."

That's the split: some people use death as an excuse to shrink, others use it as fuel.

But death isn't just terror, it's also *sublime.*

Every mystical tradition knew this. That's why the French call an orgasm *la petite mort*: "the little death." It's a momentary obliteration of control. And we chase it. We ache for it. Look at how much effort goes into getting that five-second sensation—especially men. Why?

Because part of us *wants* to disappear, as we are all *ultimately* destined to do. To escape the burden of identity, obligation, and time.

In the Greek myth, *The Odyssey*, Odysseus found himself in a similar predicament. The Cyclops had trapped him and his warriors in a cave. Odysseus didn't kill the Cyclops; he blinded it. And he escaped by telling the Cyclops that his name was "No-one." It was this very same brief moment of no-identity that saved Odysseus and his men... the moment we're in now... the gap in time between "old you" and "new you."

We don't just fear death; we unconsciously eroticize it. And if even pleasure contains a shadow of death, then maybe it's not the end we're running from, after all. Maybe it's what we're always trying to taste without having to commit.

But you already are committed to death.

Every birth certificate comes with a death certificate stapled to the back of it—the only thing missing is a date.

It's what you slip in between those two documents that counts.

Marcus Aurelius said: "It is not death that a man should fear, but he should fear never beginning to live."

Because what most people call a fear of dying is really something else: a fear that they haven't done anything worth dying *for*. That they'll reach the end and realize they wished they'd played instead of spectating. So...

Train for death, not so you can die, but so you finally learn how to *live* unafraid.

If we can face the fear of death, if we can outlast its invitation, we can easily face the inevitable adversity ahead of us.

Adversity as rocket fuel

Expect adversity as surely as you expect death. Meet it with supreme boldness—see it as a test of skill.

Napoleon Hill said, "The majority of people begin to drift as soon as they meet with opposition, and not one out of ten thousand will keep on trying after failing two or three times."

Drifting is what happens when you can't take the punch. Destination: back to the Vanishing Point loop.

Encountering adversity means you are moving towards what you want.

If you're *not* encountering adversity, it means you're drifting. The greater the adversity, the greater the goal you have set.

Fear of adversity freezes us to the spot. And the greatest fear is social adversity—an ancient fear of rejection from the collective. It's the fear that people will see you slip before you rise. That they'll laugh. That they'll say, "See? I told you not to try."

Pity those people.

They don't have the guts to do what you want to do. They're spectators who secretly want to be players.

A tired analogy in the personal development space is the crabs in a bucket scenario. We're told that if you put a bunch of crabs in a bucket and one of them tries to climb out, the other crabs pull that crab back down. Supposedly, this reflects human nature.

It's poetic, but wrong.

That's humans projecting how *they* act onto crabs (and from the previous chapter we know that animals do not possess the same type of subjective, storytelling consciousness as humans do: "Look, that crab's trying to escape. What, does he think he's better than me? Drag that bastard back down!").

Crabs in a bucket don't pull each other down out of malice. They're just panicking. Flailing. Trying to climb anything they can reach—which makes it *appear* they are dragging down a crab that tries to escape.

And people? Not so different.

The difference is that we call our panic wisdom. We wrap our fear in advice, warnings, sarcasm, getting ducks in a row, anything that makes it sound noble. But underneath, it's the same: disoriented minds grabbing at anything they can reach.

Most people aren't trying to keep you down. They're just terrified of what your rise reveals about their own *sub*-mission.

I once had a client who was a glamorous, young, single woman struggling with her weight. It had been the cause of a life-threatening stroke that she was only now recovering from, after months of speech and physical therapy.

We worked through her Deleted Scene and her Vanishing Point. I explained her behavioral genetics (something we will get to tomorrow): who she truly was and what she was put here to do. We planned a natural health regime to fortify her while she figured out how to live.

The weight began to fall off. She started to regain her health and her confidence. The destructive cycle of binge-eating—a response to her previously unexamined sadness—ground to a halt and slowly began to spiral upwards. It was a pleasure to watch her inherent sparkle re-ignite. Her father—who she lived alone with—thanked me profusely.

Then her "friends" got involved. Her "friends" were also overweight, she explained. And now they were saying things to her like, "Oh, you looked better when you had more curves, girl!" "Like, don't lose too much weight, it's not attractive."

Her "friends" effectively tried to kill her. They were panicked crabs in her bucket, I explained. She saw through it and moved on without them. She replaced her "friends" with authentic ones—nothing to do with their weight—just friends who cared about her and supported her vision for a healthier life.

And the adversity only strengthened her resolve.

So, expect this kind of adversity. Understand where it comes from, and pity the poor, panicked "crabs."

We fear criticism because we crave approval. We crave approval because we aren't sure of who we are and why we're here (it keeps coming back to that, doesn't it?). But:

Criticism is more about the person criticizing.

Ever wonder who writes those one-star reviews for gas stations?

It's a gas station. You pump gas and leave. Who cares?! As if, when we're low on gas, we say, "Yeah, honey, I checked the reviews on that gas station. They're *bad*. Let's Uber home."

Who does that? It's them! Those crabs.

They're not reviewing. They're venting. Same with the trolls, the whiners, the failed wannabes, the bitter critics—they're just digital crabs, flailing for control.

Such people have always been around, but the internet gave them a microphone, and now they're making up for lost time by spewing their venom on anything and everything (usually in places where people can't fight back).

It's the same thing for compulsive whiners. Get ready for them, especially when in business. If I was selling twenty-dollar bills for ten dollars each, I guarantee some clown would complain because his arrived creased.

Find the defiance within to see all adversity as a red rag to a bull.

Do not give energy to the obstacle. Take energy *from* the obstacle.

Treat all adversity as rocket fuel.

And enjoy it.

That's right, *enjoy it*. Rewards don't feel like rewards without struggle. As Seneca said, "No man is more unhappy than he who never faces adversity. For he is not permitted to prove himself."

Marcus Aurelius explained it somewhat cryptically: "That which rules within... when the fire is strong, it soon appropriates to itself the matter which is heaped upon it, and consumes it, and rises higher by means of this very material."

When the fire is strong enough inside you, adversity gets burned up by it. Adversity becomes *fuel* when you see through the hidden panic of others who don't dare as you do.

So, be ready. Commit.

A Roman strategist named Vegetius famously wrote "Igitur qui desiderat pacem, praeparet bellum." Translated:

"Therefore, let him who desires peace, prepare for war."

He wrote this when he saw Rome getting soft. Rome ignored him. Around a century later, Rome fell.

Adversity isn't the problem. Unpreparedness for it is.

The goal isn't to avoid the battle.

It's to become the one who's ready for it.

Praepara Bellum
(Prepare for War)

What do you think you're worth?

Let's quantify it.

Find a hill, any size hill, ideally a natural one, but concrete or synthetic is fine. Go alone. Take a pencil and paper with you, plus a glass jar.

Walk up that hill and seat yourself at the peak. Take in the view. This is *your* hill.

Now, draw a horizontal line across the paper. On the far left, write the number one. On the far right, write the number ten. This is a scale of 1-10.

Now, on the left side, draw a vertical scale for all the things you want. Relationships, career, wealth, health, your call. Write them from top to bottom.

Now score marks for each item 1-10: Point A and Point B. Point A is where you are now with those things—give that a score of 1-10. Point B is where you would like to be for those things—give that a score of 1-10. Plot all this on the paper.

Next, place that completed piece of paper into the glass jar.

Done that? Good. Now, if *anything* for Point B scored less than 10...

... take out that box of matches I gave you and...

You know the drill. Watch it burn inside that glass jar.

When the fire has cleansed you and exhausted itself, put the lid on that jar. You're going to keep those ashes in a sacred place when you get home.

But before you go down the hill, read this oath *aloud:*

THE OATH ON THE HILL

I do not measure myself anymore.

I have destroyed the scale.

That jar held my limits, not my worth.

That paper was not my potential. It was my cage.

I climbed this hill not to find clarity, but to bury fear.

To kill the story that told me I had to earn permission.

That told me I had to be liked, ready, qualified, safe.

I am not here to be safe.

I am here to be reforged into something stronger.

From this moment forward:

I do not ask, "Am I enough?"

I ask, "What must be done?"

I will walk without the old armor.

I will act without fallback.

I will fight without Plan B.

This is the hill I die on.

And that's why I will not die today.

Photocopy that oath and stick it to the jar of ashes. You will return to this hill when the job is done. Not to reflect. But to confirm the commitment you made on this day.

It would've been poetic to report that I got a rematch with the giant I backed away from, but we weren't to cross swords with the Telford Tigers again that season. In any case, this wasn't about revenge. It wasn't personal—that giant was just being a hockey player. A real one.

I had no goal other than standing up and not backing down. It was about honor and code.

It was about pushing adversity back across the line in the sand.

And I was ready.

I worked out to build muscle and gain weight. I punched bags as much as I skated. I memorized the techniques Toronto and Calgary taught me. And I played a much more physical game. I hit when I didn't need to hit. I squared up to players who shoved me.

But nobody wanted to fight.

I was starting to get penalties for the provocation, my game was suffering, and the coach almost benched me because of it. So, I had to "dial it down" and wait for the redemption I craved.

Finally, with just two games to go that season, my time came, in a tense match against Swindon Wildcats. I did what I'd been doing a lot of lately: ramming players into the boards as hard and fast as I could. And finally, someone took the bait...

We were still up close when he dropped the gloves.

I dropped mine.

Here we go...

The training Toronto and Calgary gave me? Yeah, all that went to hell. I got all emotional and swung...

I missed and spun around like an off-balance figure skater.

No...!

But my opponent didn't hit back. He hesitated—maybe puzzled by my sudden audition for the national figure skating team.

So... as I came around, I stuck my fist out.

I jammed my back skate into the ice. The energy from my spin thrust my fist straight into his nose.

I felt it crack. I heard him yell.

I grabbed his jersey, just like Calgary showed me.

The other guy held his nose with one hand and threw a half-hearted jab with the other. It bust my lip.

I pounced on him as if I was a raging lion, tipping him onto his back, my angry claws jammed into his body armor.

I took a punch to the eye.

On top of him and on all fours, I kept pounding his face. I'd never seen so much blood. His nose had exploded.

In the end, it took two referees just to pull me off the poor guy.

The crowd roared. No popcorn-rain.

It was over.

The referees dragged me away towards the penalty box like I was being arrested for murder. Rock music burst out over the speaker.

I spun my head around. Calgary and Toronto had been watching from behind; they were slapping their sticks on the ice proudly with wry smiles on their faces. My teammates were slapping their sticks against the boards in approval.

My bloodied right hand was shaking. I glanced up at the timer. My penalty would run over the game time remaining.

Thank. God.

I haughtily took my seat in the penalty box as if it was a reclaimed throne. Then my bloody baptism was announced on the arena speakers: "Number two, James Sheridan, five-minute penalty for fighting." The crowd roared like they'd won something sacred, electrifying the air, even though we were about to lose the actual game.

My face stung and my hand throbbed. And my lip had bled over the front of my jersey—rosy stains on the team colors of white, blue, and gold. I scraped a sliver of frost from one of my skates and pressed it against my left eye with my hand.

Vanessa—my first love—scurried toward the penalty box, and her innocent face scanned her one-eyed boyfriend from behind the plexiglass. "Are you okay!?" she shouted, her voice competing with the crowds as she pressed her palm against the transparent wall between us.

"You should see the other guy," I joked, holding my left eye, smiling with a thumbs-up from my spare hand.

And in the same moment, I *did* see the "other guy." He sat across the ice directly opposite me, like a reflection.

My bloody twin.

Except he was flanked by a medic holding a device like some kind of ventilator, and a crying woman I imagined was his wife. The situation appeared much worse than it first seemed.

I had done that.

The 1987/8 season was my last ever.

Find the lion, lose the pride.

Before we create our vision tomorrow, let's sleep on this: we must be sure we don't do the right things for the wrong reasons, or the wrong things for the right reasons.

And remember, things rarely go according to plan, no matter how well you have your "ducks in a row." But when you act, the world must react, for good or bad. And then you adjust. Ready, fire, aim—recalibrate while moving.

I reached the top of the hill, grabbed my packed lunch and walked over to where that castle was supposed to be.

I imagined this castle being full of visitors, but I was the only one there. Then I saw why:

It was a façade—it was only a wall.

Confused, I marched closer. It was indeed old, built in 1762. But it was fake. A folly built for some guy who wanted to enhance his view from the town below. It even had a name—an appropriate name: *Sham Castle.*

Sitting against the solitary castle wall, taking in its stone and iron, shaking my head in amazement as I ate my lunch, I digested the day.

Something General Patton once said took on new meaning: "Fixed fortifications are monuments to the stupidity of mankind."

I realized I had to go back to America. There would be plenty of time to come back to England and stare at the sea when I was old. Right now, I had important work to do.

I had an oath to swear.

Walking through the stone arch at the center of the façade, I took a picture of myself in this spot to remember the moment of clarity. The declaration seemed etched onto my face as I stared at myself on the screen. I scooped some earth from the foot of *Sham Castle* and placed it in the empty lunch bag. One day I would return to this hill and put it back—when the job is done.

Now it was time to figure out exactly what that job would be.

It's time for you to figure that out, too.

Prepare to commit. To swear an oath that renders fear redundant.

Failure becomes temporary and even *necessary* the moment you view it as the price of entry, not the end of the game.

Forget past failure. Your best shot is the *next* shot.

Take it.

DAY **6**

GET YOUR FIX

Spoiled for choice

"You can be anything."

That's what we're told.

And it's 100% true. I'm not saying that to be kind or aligned; I'm saying it because I know the truth of it first-hand (and the personal cost of living that truth).

Let me repeat, so you understand me very clearly before continuing: *You 100% CAN be ANYTHING.*

It's true.

It's also overwhelming.

Too many options lead to paralysis. Sure, we can be anything. So we often end up *not* being anything. Without an inner compass, too many choices are disorienting.

But we must strive for something. Why?

We are capable of anything, but each of us is especially wired for something specific, and until we find and embrace that *specific* thing, we feel disconnected, regardless of how "successful" we are by other measures.

We are built for a purpose. If an object does not serve a purpose, we correctly deem it "pointless." The same applies to humans...

If *we* do not serve a purpose, *life* feels "pointless."

I believe this is the root cause of anxiety and depression today. We feel pointless on the surface as we navigate a superficial world of serfdom. But deep down, something is screaming at us to the contrary. Drugs and alcohol only muffle the screaming, making it even louder when the effects wear off.

The value systems forced on us clearly aren't working. Most people are lost at sea. Look around:

A 2017 survey by DHM Research found that two-thirds of Americans do not have a written life plan (DHM Research 2017). Research by psychologist John Norcross shows that about 46 percent of people maintain their New Year's resolutions at six months.

Most people lie on surveys (Tourangeau and Yan, 2007), so it's probably even worse.

As if we needed the proof to know all this—most of us embody it. These aren't just statistics. They're tragedy in numbers. A tragedy that begs the questions:

How can we expect life *not* to be pointless if we don't *give* it a point?

How can we expect to get to a destination if we don't *know* what that destination is?

And even if we do know the destination, how can we ensure we *get there?*

What exactly do you want? What is your destination? And most importantly:

What is it that lights you up inside so much, that reaching your destination becomes inevitable?

All these questions point to one root question. The question humans have asked for thousands of years, and still seem unable to answer:

Who am I and why am I here?

This is the question we must and shall *definitively* answer. Answer that question—*The Question*—correctly, and your destination not only zooms into focus, but you also become so charged with energy to accomplish it that motivation, commitment, and resilience become *automatic.*

Your answer to *The Question* is your oath on autopilot.

And today will not end until you're sworn to it.

A famous attempt to answer *The Question* also became a foundational piece of modern psychology. Abraham Maslow—the psychologist who dared to ask what humans could become—phrased it as the human need for what he called "self-actualization."

It was a noble start, and it's been parroted and distorted for decades, but even Maslow himself admitted the limitations of it both in the paper itself and in a later work. But I believe Maslow provided us with an important clue when he said (emphasis mine):

"A musician must make music, an artist must paint, a poet must write *if he is to be ultimately at peace with himself.*"

He went on:

"Self-actualization refers to the desire for self-fulfillment, namely the *tendency* for the individual to become actualized in what he *is* potentially."

So he implies that the answer to *The Question* is already *within us* and *always was*.

He later referred to it as, "what comes naturally and easily out of one's own *nature*, one's constitution, one's *biological fate or destiny*." This implies the answer to *The Question* is baked into our biological cake.

Nietzsche would add: "Become what thou *art*!"

Maslow and Nietzsche were not alone in this conclusion, as we will see shortly.

So, the self-actualization map is instantly available to us by looking within. But how to use that map to pinpoint one's purpose has remained a mystery to this day. It would require what Maslow called "special hunting techniques."

So, let's go hunting.

Get your fix

It was hard to believe my flight back to the States was tomorrow. I would make today count—I wouldn't return without my new vision mentally playing in high-definition.

And I knew exactly where to spend the day to be alone with my thoughts: Stonehenge.

Before leaving for my destination, I flicked through the photo album—my latest daily ritual. 1992...

While studying psychology and history at college, I had decided to become an airline pilot. Becoming an airline pilot would make me "successful," I thought.

I applied to the Royal Air Force, thinking that after my service I could get direct entry to the airlines. But my eyesight wasn't 20/20, so I was rejected. I tried to get into the airlines via their sponsored cadet program. But in 1992, Britain was still in the grip of a severe recession, and none of the airlines were hiring or sponsoring pilots for their training.

There was only one path to the airlines remaining: to pay for my own training and Commercial Pilot's license.

The sweetener was that the training was much cheaper in America due to the lower fuel costs, and the USA flight school would get me a visa to live and work in America. For some inexplicable reason, America had always called to me since my first vacation in Florida as a child (being allowed to eat dessert—a.k.a. pancakes—for breakfast may have had something to do with it), so I saw this as my ticket to live there, as well as realizing my ambition of becoming a pilot.

So, I worked, saved, begged, and borrowed. And by summer of 1992 I was attending a dusty, rural flight school in Tennessee. My American adventure was underway.

But it was hectic. Flight time was money, and all the students needed to build their hours with solo cross-country flights. As one plane landed, another pilot would be waiting to take over the controls. Many other Brits were there, and we would sit in camp chairs next to the taxiway, chatting, sunbathing, and drinking tea while we waited for a plane to "make it back." All we needed was a Labrador and a gramophone, a few bullet holes, and it would've looked like a scene from The Battle of Britain.

There were strict rules: Be back before sunset. No closer than 500 feet from the ground unless landing. No entering the "forbidden zones."

Whatever.

We got so bored with cross-country flights in those slow training aircraft, we would fly through canyons, under bridges, in formation, and right through "forbidden zones," all as I listened to Depeche Mode's *Violator* album over the intercom. And if that got old, we would climb as high as possible, then stall and spin the plane back down to the deck.

But one day, the shenanigans got the better of me. Returning from one of my cross-country trips, somewhere over Kentucky, a cloud layer appeared and I became "temporarily unsure of my position."

In other words, I was lost.

It's an old aviation joke that pilots never say they're lost; they're just "temporarily unsure of their position." In aviation, it's a joke. When it comes to answering *The Question*, it's for real.

You're not lost. You're just "temporarily unsure of your position."

In both aviation and life, the first step is to get a fix on your position. To find what is real and what is not.

Where do we stand right now? What are we dealing with?

That's what I reminded myself of, as I sat on a bench at Stonehenge. Spring equinox was looming, and the sun kept dodging shifting gray clouds to get a peek at the enigmatic monoliths. Tourists reverently circled it, their voices low, as if in a church. The tranquility and mystery. The things those stones must have seen. I couldn't help thinking of Arthurian legend whenever I visited this place.

I'd brought a packed hot lunch, and I was settled for the day. I had my notepad and pencils handy, and an umbrella just in case. It was time to plot a course on the self-actualization map. It was time to create my vision.

Not a "goal." Not a "mission." And definitely not an "affirmation..."

A *vision*.

It was time to answer *The Question*. Let's answer it for you at the same time.

So, there are two parts to *The Question*:

1. **Who am I?**

2. **Why am I here?**

We must answer them in that order. To know why you're here—your purpose in life—is a result of answering the first question: Who am I?

When you have a *true, distinctive, instructive, and detailed* answer to the first question, the answer to the second question reveals itself.

Definitively answering the most important question any human can ever ask themselves deserves two separate parts.

Part One: Who are you?

There is only one truth about who you are. In reality, truth is truth, there are no "versions" of truth. So there are not several overlapping versions or pieces of a puzzle you have to put together.

Just *one* truth.

It got steadily buried since birth, and humans have sensed as much for as long as they've been conscious, or our myths wouldn't exist.

Strip away the swords, the gods, the robes, the miracles, and you'll see it. Every myth that survived this long carries the same hidden instruction manual:

There is a deeper self which is hidden beneath the social mask. It must be found. And catastrophe is often the catalyst that begins the quest to find it.

- Arthur must lose Camelot to glimpse the soul
- Buddha must renounce the palace to awaken under the tree
- Moses must leave Egypt to meet his destiny
- Gilgamesh must bury his friend to learn he's not a god

Each begins with an inherited identity. Each is shattered by truth. Each must walk through trial, exile, and death.

And only what is real survives the crucible.

But it's worth it. Discovering the true Self, it is written, is the ultimate prize.

A treasure we must pursue—not as a luxury, but as a *duty*.

As Jung's protégé, Erich Neumann observed, "The mythological theory of foreknowledge also explains the view that all knowing is 'memory.' Man's task in the world is to remember with his conscious mind what was knowledge before the advent of consciousness."

Perhaps the richest legend is King Arthur, the Grail, and the knights of the round table. The Grail isn't a chalice; it's a metaphor. The quest for the Grail is a quest to find what was lost: the Divine *within*— perhaps an ancient way of describing the true Self now hidden within us.

To reach the Grail, each knight had to face himself. The test was spiritual. Most failed. Only one—Galahad—was pure enough to pass the test. The others were shattered by what they could not reconcile within. All but one failed to answer The Question.

The Grail, once found, vanished. It could not remain in a world not yet ready. But it is said, Arthur waits in Avalon, and will return when he is called by those who seek the Grail.

As Grail legend tells us, the discovery of who you truly are is hard to attain.

Perhaps you already know how difficult it is to find a *true, distinctive, instructive, and detailed* answer to who you *truly* are. You may find fragments of truth here and there, or see traits that apply to us all, but offer no clues about your true purpose in life.

And there's a reason for that…

Let's agree that the "true Self" simply means the version of you that's original, authentic, and not shaped by what the world has trained you to be—*the unconditioned version of you.*

And if "unconditioned" is our benchmark, there's only one place in a human life that meets that standard: birth.

Birth is the closest point we ever experience to being our true self. It's the moment before the world starts shaping us, labeling us, or training us (this is why many cultures elevate children above adults; because they see them as nearer to truth itself—uncorrupted, untrained, and still in their original form).

At birth, what exists is *biological* (even the fetus in the womb is considered biological).

Therefore, the true Self is biological.

After birth, that biological self becomes contaminated with a *biographical* self. Social conditioning starts shaping our behavior, which obviously obscures what would be the pure and natural behavior of the true Self.

Think of it this way:

Music = your true self

Speakers = your behavior

The music and the speakers are not the same thing.

Poor quality speakers will muffle or disguise the pure sound of your inner "music."

The quality of your "speakers" is a measure of how much social conditioning distorted your true Self.

And unless you were raised in perfect conditions, nobody's "speakers" are perfect quality.

That's why it's so hard for us to discover our true self. The sound of our pure inner music is compromised by speaker quality, or social conditioning.

The pure form of the music exists, but we usually can't hear it clearly. It sounds distant.

So we turn to personality tests for answers. And they have two systemic failures that let us down as tools to answer *The Question*:

System Failure #1: Personality tests do not measure personality.

When most people take a personality test, I think it's fair to say they are trying to discover their "true self" or what would be the point of taking it?

And we have already agreed that the true self is biological.

If all we care about is a person's attempt to find who they truly are, then the only thing that matters is the version of them that existed *before* the world began shaping them.

And that means the only valid target of a personality system is the biological self, not the biographical one.

But unless you can give such a test to a newborn (the biological self), personality tests can only measure what a person has become after social conditioning (the biographical self).

In short, personality tests can only measure behavior—deleted scenes and scar-scripts included. They can only listen to the "speakers," not the actual "music."

Psychology will argue that behavior correlates with personality, but correlation is not causation, and it is certainly not identity. That's like saying the music and the speakers are the same thing.

And because of this fact...

Personality psychology commits what's called a "category error."

A category error happens when you treat a thing as belonging to the wrong kind of thing.

Here's the contradiction:

Psychology now quietly admits that personality is biological ("music").

But it measures personality with tools that measure behavior ("speakers").

That is a category error. And here is the consequence of that:

If personality psychology keeps its definition, its tests become invalid; if it keeps its tests, its definition becomes false. Either way, the field collapses.

We don't need to burn this one down because it burns itself down with its own definitions.

So put the matches away and read the American Psychology Association's (APA) *own definition* of personality to further the point (this is the first line of a suspiciously long definition, emphasis mine):

"The *enduring* configuration of characteristics and behavior that comprises an individual's unique *adjustment to life*."

Read *their own* definition closely and you'll see the contradiction. In one sentence, the APA makes personality both the thing that adjusts and the thing that determines adjustment—a recursive loop.

Psychology defines personality as two things at once:

1. **"Enduring characteristics"**

2. **A person's "adjustment to life"**

Those two ideas cannot coexist.

If something is *enduring*, it isn't shaped by circumstance. If something is an *adjustment*, it isn't prior to behavior.

A thing cannot be both the cause and the consequence of itself.

And that's why personality tests don't measure personality.

They measure post-conditioning behavior and then call it "you." These are not "personality tests." They are post-conditioning "behavior tests."

The music is there, which is why you *might* sense some truth in a personality test result, but it's corrupted to some degree or even plain wrong. And even then, what you think is the truth about yourself may not be the truth, *because these tests are impossible to fail; everyone gets a result by default, however compromised the fit.*

If the true self = the unconditioned self, and the least conditioned moment of human life = biological birth, then personality tests (which measure behavior after conditioning) cannot measure the true self.

Next let's look at just how bad the sound on their "speakers" is:

System Failure #2: Most personality tests—make that *behavior* tests—weren't even built for you; they were built for "them."

By "them," I mean corporations and institutions. They have their own agenda, and it doesn't usually match yours.

The most used tests—such as Myers-Briggs Type Indicator (MBTI) and variants derived from it—were designed to classify you. To slot you into a team. And its reliability is now widely criticized.

Here's the thing about the Myers-Briggs test:

Jung never built a personality test.

His *Psychological Types* was a map of inner energy flows—intuition, thinking, feeling, sensation—not a questionnaire.

But in the 1940s, Katharine Briggs and her daughter Isabel Myers took Jung's ideas and industrialized them. They were not psychologists. They simply built a tool that was intended to place women in wartime factory jobs more efficiently. Jung's types became four binary switches—introvert or extrovert, sensing or intuitive, thinking or feeling, judging or perceiving.

That last one, "Judging or Perceiving," wasn't Jung's idea at all— they added it themselves to make their typology fit the workplace.

This addition spuriously doubled the number of Jung's types to sixteen, muddying the waters even more, and doing the exact thing Jung cautioned against doing in his work.

Jung's own writings make the point clearly. He said his typology was "not in any sense to be regarded as a system of classification in the usual sense," and separately warned that it would be "a great mistake" to treat his types as rigid categories.

After the war, corporate America fell in love with it. It made people sortable. The test spread through management consulting, education, and even the military.

The irony is that *Jung believed personality was innate, that it is biological.* But the MBTI stripped out everything organic and replaced it with a grid of letters.

But we look at our test result and think, "Well, it must be right if Fortune 500 companies use it!" So we invent a narrative to fit it—a Vanishing Point—so it feels real. For a while.

The Enneagram is another example of the confusion: it's a spiritual self-help tool from the 1970s that got repackaged as psychology—with types based on childhood trauma and fear—by definition making it about biography, not biology.

So, to answer *The Question*, we must dig deeper.

Literally.

Reflecting, I stared at the altar stone at Stonehenge, hearing the whisper of a 22-year-old pilot trying to find his way home: "Get a fix on current position, get a fix on current position..."

My notepad was empty, but my mind was full. Ideas sparking.

Time for lunch to help the process: reheated shepherd's pie. I forked out hearty mouthfuls and devoured it while staring into the ancient stone circle as rain clouds rolled in. I felt invisible to the tourists.

A mind without a purpose-aligned vision is a trouble magnet, I thought, struggling not to scold myself for being lost to a scar-script for the past few years.

I'd always had such a driving vision, and I'd always accomplished it. But only now I realized, I hadn't set myself a new vision since the last one was realized, several years ago. So, I had drifted, steadily, one degree at a time, until I was lost. Until I crashed and burned.

Not this time.

Now I would lay out my new vision...

I already knew the answer to the first part of *The Question* (Who am I?) for myself. And I knew it for any client who I'd worked with one-on-one. Watching the client's jaw drop as I revealed their answer to the first part of *The Question* never grew old.

If you were one-on-one with me now, I would answer the first part of *The Question* for you in under five minutes.

How?

Because of the personality system I invented and used successfully for years. In stark contrast to the legacy personality systems explained earlier, I have found that my system:

1. Is enduring and consistent throughout a person's life. Whether the subject is 5 or 55, the type is clear, although obviously a lot clearer in the young because they are closer to the true Self.

2. Focuses on finding who a person truly is and *always was underneath the surface*, not a muddy cocktail of surface traits. It exposes biography to be as much of an influence on an individual as a sauce is to a steak—superficial and easily scraped off—yet it gives the *appearance* of being different, special.

3. Is designed for individuals, not institutions. The romantic application is game-changing, as true pairings become obvious as well as obvious mechanisms to make existing relationships work.

4. Has highly distinctive types, each one shockingly different from one another, yet each individual shockingly alike within that same type group.

5. Appears to have ancient origins, each type almost like its own tribe. Yet, when all types were imagined working together, a formidable team is revealed.

6. Shows how each type has an inherent drama, like a problem that must be solved, a journey that must be taken.

7. Allows a fast way to identify the types, and how often they repeat their cycles.

8. Holds up consistently across cultures, nationalities, age, sex, and race.

9. Reveals and explains the hidden and repeating cycles in all aspects of people's lives.

10. *Acts as a clear signpost to finding the purpose of each of the types.* It naturally needs to answer the all-important second part of *The Question*.

In short, my system answers *The Question*, and then some.

There's just one problem: you're *not* one-on-one with me now.

My personality system and how it transformed people and gave them purpose was my *passion* (and there was the big clue), but it was limited to being used only with people I was in direct contact with. It was like a sword that required expert handling—only by me. For if the wrong type was assigned—by force-fitting, as every personality test does—that would be disastrous.

Bad information is worse than no information.

And that would make it as flawed as all those other personality systems, I told myself. But then something I said yesterday barged into my thoughts, with a "Hypocrite" neon sign flashing above it: "If you have nothing better to replace it with, you're no better than the things you burned."

I shook my head at the implication this was taking me to. There was another good reason why I'd so far resisted turning my system into a mainstream personality test:

System Failure #3: People lie on personality tests (Viswesvaran & Ones, 1999, Paulhus & Reid, 1991, Griffith & Peterson, 2008).

As I explained earlier, this is where we mistake the speakers for the music. It's called "self-report bias" (Paulhus & Vazire, 2007).

Nurturing, deleted scenes, scar-scripts, and social conformity synthesize a personality mask—a mash-up of shifting surface traits that *feels* unique, but also hides the true Self underneath.

And the person taking the test is usually wearing their mask.

In short, people lie. Not deliberately. The person taking the test absolutely believes who they think they are, and that the answers they're giving are all true. And the older we get, the harder it gets to find the truth buried under years of rubble.

It takes an uncommon level of emotional maturity and/or desire to be honest with oneself to answer personality tests truthfully. Even more so when a user is allowed to choose from a selection of profiles...

I recalled how I'd witnessed this myself many times in early experiments with my system. When presented with all the profiles, people would sometimes say they see themselves in all the types (usually picking all the best parts from each type!) or none of them or the one they'd like to be the most or the one that most aligns with their vocation. Pure nonsense!

Later on, when one-on-one, I would reveal their true profile. Their longtime spouse would laugh in astonishment and back me up, and the subject, often pleasantly stunned, would agree and own it. But there were other times when the result was so unsettling that the subject threw a panicked tantrum because they also saw their type's dark side when the mirror was held up.

So I had learned it was far better to simply tell each client the answer to *The Question*, never revealing my system to anyone. But I now realized certain problems with that approach had weighed me down, and were ultimately partly responsible for my fall:

1. I found one-on-one work to be personally draining (you probably gathered as much by now). As I said on Day 4, most people don't really want to heal; they just want permission to keep reading their scar-script. Which is good for the billing cycle, but not good for sleeping at night.

2. One-on-one work is not a scalable business. I could only be in one place at a time.

Third, and I hated to admit it, I just didn't want people messing up my precious creation and complaining that it didn't work when I knew full well it did—*if* the subject discovered their true type.

"No way," I said to myself, taking the last bite of my lunch.

Or was there a way?

I'd always had a gift for seeing patterns in things that most other people didn't see—when I was a kid, it used to freak my mother out. Perhaps I could see a pattern today, or at least some guidance born of one.

I allowed a random current of thoughts to flow through me, inviting a deeper source to participate...

I scanned the circle of monoliths.

Originally, its form was a circle of thirty stone archways that I believed to be solar "gates." This would mean each gate would represent the number 12 in order to make a circle: 360 degrees of a circle divided by 30 solar gates = 12.

The number 12 has repeating significance that runs through humanity as a structure of completion, of wholeness to function. *But only* when 2 regulating forces—often a symbolic male and female—were added, to make 14—the same number of types in my personality system. And each of the 14 (12+2) had a distinctly different personality or purpose:

- 12 months + 2 symbolic regulators (Summer and Winter Solstices)

- 12 Knights of the Round Table plus 2 symbolic regulators (Arthur and Guinevere)

- 12 Olympians plus 2 symbolic regulators (Zeus and Hera)

- 12 disciples plus 2 symbolic regulators (Jesus and the Holy Spirit)

- 12 Imams plus 2 symbolic regulators (Muhammad and Fatima—revered figures of the lineage)

- 12 tones of Western music plus 2 symbolic regulators (the Octave and the Fundamental)

- 12 animals of the Chinese Zodiac plus 2 symbolic regulators (Yin and Yang)

- 12 meridians in Chinese medicine plus 2 symbolic regulators (Ren Mai & Du Mai)

- 12 Tribes of Israel plus 2 symbolic regulators (Yahweh and the Priestly Tribe of Levi)

- 12 cranial nerves plus 2 symbolic regulators (the Brainstem and the Cerebrum)

- 12 types plus 2 symbolic regulator types in my personality system

Then there was the zodiac...

Zodiac. I couldn't help but admire its resilience and "stickiness" among people.

Now *there* was a personality system that didn't suffer from self-report bias. People are simply *told* what personality they are based on their birthdate, and then they just have to deal with it, however much it felt to them like ramming a square peg into a round hole.

I liked that part. The rest? Not so much.

But, today, in this location, something about this line of thought pulled me deeper.

I decided to go with it...

When it comes to biology and biography, by implication, the zodiac defines itself as neither (birth is not its defining factor—birth *date* is). And pulling it apart is embarrassingly easy. There are many angles the critique could take (such as thousands of years of planetary precession means all the birthdates are wrong by at least one star sign shift, it's based on the view of constellations from ancient Babylon—modern day Iraq, the Barnum Effect, etc.), but this one is perhaps the most obvious:

If personality is defined by birthdate, how can two people be born minutes apart, or a few miles apart either side of the International Date Line, and have completely different personalities?

They can't.

It's a biological absurdity. And we've established that *true* Self is biological.

"Cusps" and "Houses" et al will be used as defense mechanisms and system patches, even scar-scripts, but these were all part of the misinterpretations of the ancient truth about the zodiac.

Around 3000 years ago, Babylonians created a star map that split the sky into twelve sections. It was for the purposes of agricultural predictions and omens—a cosmic calendar.

And it had nothing to do with personality types.

Meanwhile, ancient Greece had fully established a 12+2 structure of their gods, each with distinct personalities and purposes.

I believe the Greeks had projected their own enduring personalities—as well as the inherent talents and dramas of each type—onto their gods.

Around 2,300 years ago, Alexander conquered Babylon and cultural exchange between Greece and Babylon began. The Babylonian star map then found its way back to Greece.

And here's where the waters became muddied...

When the Greeks absorbed and translated this star system, they did so through their own cultural filter—one that had already begun to project human traits onto gods.

As a result, the zodiac became psychologized.

What began as a sacred cosmological system for Babylonians was twisted into personality projection by the Greeks, then later corrupted by gossip and charlatans in Roman forums, its remnants buried by the Dark Ages.

It might've been forgotten, but in 1930, Princess Margaret's birth led to a horoscope for her being published in the Sunday Express newspaper, reigniting public fascination. Suddenly, horoscopes became fashionable again, rebranded for the masses, and reborn into a fortune-telling column beside the newspaper crossword. And went on to become a multi-billion dollar industry.

A foggy drizzle crept into Stonehenge.

But I asked myself as I opened my umbrella, if the zodiac was pure nonsense why has it endured so long? Why does it enjoy such fanaticism?

Here is why:

1. The fortune-telling aspect caters to the human fear of uncertainty. And most predictions are broad enough so that anyone could find the truth in them (see: The Barnum Effect), or now *look* for the predictions to come true, creating a self-fulfilling prophecy (more on this tomorrow).

2. No self-report bias. Zodiac is conveniently immunized against the biggest problem of any other personality system. People are told who they are based on their birthdate. No discussion, no window-shopping, no mood-pandering, no "I'm two types," "I'm none of the types," "I'm all of the types," etc. They're given a type, then the individual has no choice but to invent a narrative to make it fit (humans are good at that, remember?), once again creating a self-fulfilling prophecy—and a dangerous one if it sends a person down a flawed personal or professional path.

3. It offers a symbol, a flag to wave, a name, a tribal rally point.

   And finally, there it was, I realized:

4. **Sometimes the zodiac profile—*when detailed enough*— really is a true match to the individual. *When the dates just happen to line up the right way.***

I snatched up my pencil and began writing:

The zodiac profiles are shallow—symbolic shorthand rather than full identities—but their essence is surprisingly distinct. Even in their diluted form, you can feel types trying to break through.

What struck me most was this: when considering the most detailed profiles, each of the 12 signs roughly mapped onto 12 of the 14 types in my own system. A far from perfect match, but a pattern. Some mirrored my types more than others, albeit without the detailed definition of my system. Others had shared outlines.

But two were missing. The regulators, to make it a 12+2 system.

I wrote: *What regulates the zodiac? What defines it?*

The Sun. It moves through the constellations, creating the signs. It marks time.

The Moon. It governs the tides, the cycles, the pull of the internal world.

They regulate the cosmos but were never given a role with the cast of 12.

What if I corrected that?

What if I brought the Sun and Moon down from the sky and embedded them as living types—the two missing types—in the 12+2 structure of my system?

By doing that, I would also break the ancient error.

Because once the Sun and Moon are inside the system—as types, not clocks—the zodiac is unchained from time...

No more birthdates.

The Greeks made one fundamental mistake: they locked personality to the Sun's position. They mistook the measuring stick for the meaning.

But what if they were half right?

What if the 12 signs really do reflect something real that hasn't been clearly expressed yet...

...and was never supposed to be pinned to the sky?

What if we removed the dates from the zodiac?

My head lurched upwards. I stared through the fog.

I had my vision: I would offer people a kind of "Lost Zodiac."

Truth reclaimed for a new time. Destiny over dates. *Detailed, distinctive, instructive, and truthful profiles...* and unchained from birthdates.

I would give people a new symbol, a new flag to fly, a new tribal name to rally behind... one that was, at last, *true to who they were.*

Evidently, 12+2 was a universal truth that was not mine to hoard. I would give my personality system to the world. I would create a *true* personality test.

My head sunk.

But what about self-report bias?

I whacked the pencil against my right temple, then bit it.

I recalled my early experiments and experiences with the system and one-on-ones: how the test-taker doesn't see who they are, but the person who's known them the longest sees it immediately...

So, the test would encourage the user to have a long-known third-party verify their result.

The questions would have to be as few as possible but still do the job of cutting through to the biology of a person. It could take years to develop.

My note writing couldn't keep up with my thoughts. Rain or shine, I wouldn't leave this spot until I had it all down.

I felt charged. Reignited. *Alive.* I continued...

By its very nature—that my test would have to revolve around the 14 types—this would be an inversion of every other test. Every other test asked about user *behavior* and then averaged out their answers to force-fit a result. Mine would start with the types and then see which one the user was. Mine would be more like an elimination game; questions written to filter types out, not to collect opinions or moods.

Every other test gives all users a result, even if their answers are total gibberish. That's how they're set up—everybody gets a prize. But a test that cannot be failed can, by definition, give compromised or totally false results.

So, in my test there would be no force-fitting. Mine would be the only personality test people could "fail"—if their answers were not matched to one of the types—types that I knew to be as true as they are detailed. Taking self-report bias into account, I estimated around half the people who took the test would fail. So, as well as encouraging third-party verification, I would need to create a system to reroute the people who failed, perhaps with backup systems.

"The only personality test you can fail." Maybe let's go with that, I thought. And because it targeted the biological self and a user could fail the test, it would be a true personality test, not a behavior test, like everything else. This would be for people who take it seriously, not people looking for a "fun quiz."

I would also ultimately aim to get DNA proof of my system—I had already investigated the possible gene clusters that would explain each of the types. Then there could be no debate about its truth. On Day One I asked myself, "Is there a DNA test that tells us what the point of it all is?" Now, if the evidence was there, I would make one.

My system couldn't offer fortune-telling per se (nor should it), but the repeating patterns and transformation arcs for each type were so accurate it might as well have. I had found that once I knew a person's type, based on my system, I pretty much knew their past and future (guided or unguided).

This would be personal development 2.0. *Type-specific* training.

This was it. Why am *I* here? To help others find out why *they're* here.

Several years later, you can take the test I have since created at www.metageno.net/smpt-briefing or by scanning the QR code that follows. It's completely free. Just be *brutally* honest with yourself and get third party verification. Come back when you have answered the first part of *The Question*: who are you?

Next, let's figure out *your* vision. Let's answer the second part of *The Question*:

Part Two: Why are you here?

Jung said, "People don't have ideas. Ideas have people."

This "idea" is the answer to the first part of *The Question*: an entity I have termed the true Self. Its will is clear, and it won't let you be at peace (it literally won't let you be at one *with your Self*) until you serve it in a way somehow aligned with its implicit meaning shown in your Metageno type profile you should now have. It doesn't care what you or society think about its purpose, and there are plenty more bodies to occupy now and in the future if you don't comply—if you lose your "spirit."

However, thanks to our blessing (and curse) of consciousness, you also have free will. And free will is active, whereas true Self is passive—deep in the subconscious, like a sleeping giant.

You truly can be anything you want, and that may be—and often is—in blatant defiance of the true Self.

Free will gives you the choice to defy the true Self.

But it can't separate you from it.

It's as if free will is tethered to the true Self by a rubber band—it can fly off in its own direction, but sooner or later it will snap back to its origin. The limit of the rubber band's elasticity is our existential crisis—when we feel "stretched" or "disconnected."

This tension represents the conflict at the heart of modern life.

This conflict within rages until we are at one with our Self. Until we sign a "peace treaty" with it. This treaty puts free will consciousness "in flow" with the true Self.

Creating this treaty is what it means to craft your vision.

Signing this treaty is your commitment to an oath.

Living this treaty enlists the sleeping giant within—the true Self.

Sadly, most people don't have a vision, so they have no hope of realizing a vision. Sadder still, of those that do have a vision, I believe most of those visions are not aligned with the individual's true Self. I don't need data to state what we see everywhere: people stuck in careers or situations they hate because they blindly chose to serve a flawed agenda years ago.

Free will always ends up where it wants to go, even with true Self kicking and screaming from the backseat. But at what price?

Don't climb a ladder only to find that when you reach the top you propped it against the wrong wall.

Recall how I explained the difference between our future and our destiny and how we can determine our own future but not our own destiny?

Based on that, we might say:

*Free will **determines** your future.*

*True Self **reveals** your destiny (one of multiple possible futures).*

***Aligned**, they are unstoppable.*

Free will is the reason *why* we truly can be anything we wish, regardless of the destiny true Self reveals to us.

But imagine the power when true Self and free will are aligned, when they're working together instead of pulling in different directions!

What you're about to do puts you in a small and enlightened minority. You are going to create your *type-aligned* vision.

You're going to live on purpose. In *flow*.

Setting and realizing your vision can be boiled down to a simple two-step concept:

1. Find the *right* hoop to jump through.

2. Jump through it.

Get the first part right, and the second part isn't just logical, it's compelling. It's *automatic motivation*. And it's a sure thing—because you are aligned and in flow.

As Maslow—the man who made motivation famous—noted, "some behavior is not motivated, but expressive." The Bhagavad Gita agrees: "All creatures are driven to action by their own nature."

It's effortless. One *cannot help* but do the thing one's true Self wants to do. Therefore, anyone who is living in flow with the true Self becomes *literally* "*Self*-motivated," "*Self*-disciplined," a "*Self*-starter"—a "*Self*-made" person who stands proud because of it.

This is truly what it means to become "Self-actualized."

***Everyone* is a self-starter when correctly aligned.**

If you've ever been told you were not any of those things, now you might know why. That also explains why:

True Self aligned vision is also the antidote to the modern disease.

An old saying goes, "The devil finds work for idle hands." An empty or aimless mind defaults to darkness when you literally serve no purpose; when you don't serve *the* purpose you're wired for.

When we are charged with purpose, in flow and serving the greater good, the mental vacuum is filled and one simply has no time for *self-pity*, anxiety, or depression (your true Self doesn't need your pity; it's just fine!).

Life is only "pointless" when we don't give it a point.

Many people think "life is suffering"—perhaps their bastardized takeaway from pop-Buddhism or a half-baked book they've read.

But that's only half the message—the bleak half.

Buddha himself said (parentheses mine), "There is no gift better than the gift of the dharma (God-given purpose), no gift more sweet, no gift more joyful. *It puts an end to cravings and the sorrow they bring.*"

Buddha never left his message in doubt: "Both formerly and now, I teach only suffering and the *cessation of suffering.*"

In that single line lies the *whole* of Buddhism—the frank admission that life is marked by suffering, yes, *but also the promise that the Dharma is the medicine that brings it to an end.*

Life isn't suffering. It's service.

That mental shift happens when we stop making it all about ourselves and start making it all about our Self.

The subtle and crucial difference is between self-centeredness and Self-centeredness.

Hence, I refer to this as the antidote to the modern disease.

Most people aren't clinically depressed even by the dubious DSM-5 standards; they're existentially misaligned, mistaking a lack of purpose for a mental disorder.

Viktor Frankl was a licensed psychiatrist and Holocaust survivor. He was also the father of logotherapy, meaning "therapy from purpose." Which, he explained (emphasis mine),

"... defocuses all the vicious-circle formations and feedback mechanisms which play such a great role in the development of neuroses. Thus, **the typical self-centeredness of the neurotic is broken up instead of being continually fostered and reinforced**... the patient is actually confronted with and reoriented toward the meaning of his life."

It's also why addiction is rampant in modern life: meaning collapses, mindless pleasure-seeking and cravings flood in to fill the void. As Frankl observed during his time in Nazi concentration camps:

"When some gave up work and would therefore be executed within the next day, something typical occurred: they took out a cigarette... and started smoking... **Meaning had subsided, and consequently the seeking of immediate pleasure had taken over.**"

Consider that Frankl witnessed and survived the horrors of Auschwitz. Such horrors hardly compare to the "hardships" most people dwell on today. And Frankl's key observation during his imprisonment was this:

People with purpose endure.

Nietzsche echoed this when he said, "He who has a *why* to live for can bear almost any how."

This is why the concept of retirement is nonsensical to the self-actualized individual. Not only nonsensical, but deadly. How many people die shortly after retiring because they had nothing to do?

There is no "retirement" when there is no line between work and play, when you are in flow and in service. You give your gift with your final breath. A final breath, I would add, that has been greatly delayed as a result.

The gift of retirement is freedom to live a life of purpose, uncompromised by other commitments.

Perhaps you're too young for retirement to be the issue. Perhaps you're stuck in a job you hate with bills to pay and/or kids to raise, making it too hard to live your purpose?

If that's the case, I offer this:

1. Look for something in your day job that is the closest expression to your true purpose, the thing that's driving you from your Metageno type profile. Bring that into your work as much as possible. You may even find that this simple move takes you somewhere interesting, raises your enthusiasm levels, maybe gets you noticed more. *Meanwhile...*

2. Get going on a sideline that is aligned with your true Self. Technology has opened new opportunities and leveled the

playing field. Old structures are crumbling, and people are becoming more empowered.

Express your "logos" in some way, as much as possible, effortlessly and generously serving, and watch what happens within and without.

"Logos" is the Greek word to denote meaning. The search for meaning is the primary driving force in people, Frankl explained, not pleasure as many believe. He said (emphasis mine):

"This *hidden* logos of a person's existence made the difference between death and survival in some of the grimmest human trials ever known... **A human being is not one in pursuit of happiness but rather in search of *a reason* to become happy.**"

Interestingly, Maslow also used that word "hidden" in this light, implicitly and explicitly. He spoke of the "hidden bent of the individual."

And one final word from Frankl, where he elegantly confirms something I said earlier: that *we are each wired for a specific thing, something both biological and ancient...*

"These values, however, cannot be espoused and adopted by us on a conscious level—they are something that we *are*. They have crystallized in the course of our species; they are founded on our *biological past* and are rooted in our *biological depth*."

There's that word again: "Biological."

Most people confuse "purpose" with *current* work, hobbies, survival, or fantasy. But real purpose isn't random, it's *biological*. You feel it in your nervous system. It blurs the line between work and play. It shatters the concept of time.

It's what Maslow called "peak experience" and the "Flow Channel" described by Mihaly Csikszentmihalyi in 1990. It emerges when your internal structure is matched with the right function—when the job fits the frame.

This is why you can't fully self-actualize outside of your Metageno type. You can succeed. You can dominate. But you won't light up.

Flow states correlate with positive brain chemistry. These chemical markers aren't "inspiration;" they're alignment feedback.

And alignment is biological.

Without true Self alignment, people burn out chasing the wrong ideal, mistaking effort for elevation.

This is why you are not here to prove you can "become anything."

You're here to become what you always were—what you've now seen in the revealing of your Metageno Type. Especially in the part that revealed your type's "Dominant Driver."

Your Dominant Driver provides you with a true Self approved "lane" to create your vision within.

Biology refers to it as "canalization," as in canals. Think of it as a riverbed carved into your genes by evolution—you can paddle anywhere, but some routes are deeper and faster (Canalized traits are developmentally stabilized along specific pathways, often under genetic control but not dictated by simple inheritance patterns. West-Eberhard, 2003).

These lanes vary in width from one type to the next. For some types, the lanes are narrow, making it blatantly obvious what its purpose is. For other types, more exploring of the "width" is required—and that width can be surprisingly diverse. For example, the F5 "Setra" type could be equally fulfilled as a police officer or an environmental activist or an HR manager. *This is because satisfying the Dominant Driver as the common denominator is the key.*

So, using your type-specific lane or "canal," let's create your vision.

Let's start with the most important thing:

Decoupling from our inherent need to conform.

Society believes success is about prosperity, by definition. And for some types it *is*. But now, through Metageno type awareness, you can see that nothing is a one-size-fits-all deal. So:

"Success" is subjective. Every type has its own definition of success.

The dictionary and society have it wrong...

You are a "success" if you are living in flow with your true Self.

What about power? Isn't power success, also? Does being in flow also grant you power?

Let's ask the person who literally wrote the book on power, Robert Greene:

"The most intense form of self-belief is to feel a sense of destiny impelling you forward... you are liberated of the normal doubts and confusions that plague us. You have a sense of purpose that guides you but does not chain you to one way of doing things. And when your willpower is so deeply engaged, it will push you past any limits or dangers.... You now have a way of measuring what matters in life."

Let me hammer this point home, because I know from experience how those Deleted Scenes, scar-scripts, and crabs in the bucket compromise so many people.

Ralph Waldo Emerson said, "To be yourself in a world that is constantly trying to make you something else is the greatest accomplishment."

Maslow said, "Be independent of the good opinion of other people." "The most stable and therefore most healthy self-esteem is based on *deserved* respect from others rather than on external fame or celebrity and unwarranted adulation" (if only he was alive today to see the shitshow).

And even Buddha said: "Don't follow the way of the world. Wake up! Don't be lazy. Follow the right path, avoid the wrong. You will be happy here as well as hereafter... Nothing is lost in following one's own dharma (purpose), but competition in another's dharma breeds fear and insecurity."

So there is a lot to consider when choosing the right hoop to jump through. How do we ensure we don't miss anything?

As in aviation, run the checklist:

VISION CHECKLIST

Don't let pride hijack it.
If it feels performative—designed to impress others or match cultural ideals—it's probably not coming from your true Self. Drop the performance. Let your instincts lead.

Consider both strengths *and* weaknesses.
Purpose isn't just what you *can* do—it's also what you can but

probably *shouldn't*. Your weaknesses are guardrails. They rule things out. Your strengths light the way. Respect both, and you'll narrow in on what's truly yours.

Bliss is not perfection.
A life of purpose isn't a fantasy—it's a lucid one. You'll still feel pain, but it will be clean pain. Bittersweet. When you're aligned, the inner static disappears. You're no longer fighting yourself.

Imagine vividly.
Use your imagination to explore the full range of your Metageno type. Try roles on like clothes. Notice what makes your chest expand and what makes it shrink. Imagination is the scouting tool of the Self.

Accept disruption.
Sometimes purpose demands you reroute your life. That's not regression—it's correction. If you're running hard in the wrong direction, slowing down is progress. Take the one step back to leap two steps forward.

Check what's already working.
It might be right under your nose. You could already be living your purpose—just without clarity. If your current role lights you up when stripped of conformity and pressure, don't throw it out. Refine it.

Don't overlook the quiet callings.
One's "superpower" doesn't always wear a cape. It might look like caretaking, coding, organizing, or listening deeply. If it feels real and gives you peace, it counts. Truth glows quietly.

Deprioritize money.
Money is a tool, not a compass. Choosing a purpose based on income will likely backfire for most types. Let compensation follow service, not dictate it.

Time should disappear.
When you're in flow, time dilates. Your mind stops chattering. You drop into presence. Bittersweet bliss floods in. That's your signal. If your chosen path doesn't create that feeling, it's not the one.

Go beneath the badge.
Don't reduce your Metageno Type to surface traits. Your Dominant Driver that's shown on your profile is the sun in your solar system. Many expressions are possible within one type—what matters is whether your work fulfills the deep structure of your nature.

Hobbies are not *necessarily* purpose.
Liking something isn't the same as being lit up by it. Sex, food, games—they show you *how* you like to feel. Purpose shows you *who you are* when you're doing what you were made for.

Follow the golden threads.
Look back on your life. What actions pulled you in with no external reward? What made time vanish? What left you feeling more whole? These are clues. Pattern recognition is the path.

Type offers a lane, not a leash.
Your Metageno type answers *The Question* as far as your Dominant Drive goes. But if something truly beyond your type stirs your soul and feels like home, follow it (and if that is the case you might also consider if you are matched correctly with your type).

Don't downsize your dream.
If it scares you, it's probably close to the truth. You don't need to be world-class, just real. Engage your gift, and flow will follow. This is not about fantasy. This is about fit.

Take your time when crafting your type-aligned vision.

You're writing a single paragraph that will change the course of your life.

An oath you will take. A creed you will live by.

Once you know the "why" and the "who," you need to have a sense of "when."

So, next up:

SCHEDULES
and ETA

A vision isn't complete without a date by which you want to reach it. But there's a crucial balance to be aware of...

Too much pressure and we detach from flow.

Too little pressure and we risk drifting.

So, here are four laws to live by when it comes to the when:

#1: Set deadlines to force action, not betray flow.
Your vision is a private treaty between you and your Self. And it operates in *biological time*, not social time. Your milestones aren't based on what month it is. It's when alignment locks. But this also isn't an excuse to wait or to get your "ducks in a row."

#2: Make molehills out of mountains.
The trick is not to make mountains out of molehills, but to *make molehills out of mountains*. In other words, to break the big vision down into bite-sized visions, and then one day you just wake up and you're there. Baby steps, day by day, and every journey begins with a single step.

#3: Don't let tunnel-vision blind you.

A deadline should sharpen your focus, not narrow your vision. Sometimes, in chasing a date, we miss a better door opening right beside us. Stay alert to unexpected alignment. Pressure creates movement, but you still need peripheral awareness. Don't bulldoze your own evolution just to hit a number. *But* this is also not an excuse to settle or turn back!

#4: Deadlines are not the enemy, attachment to them is.

Most people fear deadlines because they think they're being judged by them. But that's backwards. Deadlines exist to create *pressure*, not punishment. Urgency is useful—it lights the fire. It brings decisions into focus and ends the false comfort of limbo. But a deadline is only a tool, it's not your judge, and it's not your master. When it becomes a scoreboard for your worth, you're no longer creating from flow. And that leads to failure.

In summary, when it comes to setting timelines for your vision and when actually working towards it, remember these words:

Pressure without punishment.

Discipline without drama.

Fire without fear.

Faith in one's Self

Tennessee, 1992. The sun was getting low. So was my fuel gauge. I reduced power and lit the strobe lights on my wingtips. The engine suddenly sounded subdued. The ground below started to look like a void that might swallow me up. If the sun went down I wouldn't be able to see the ground well enough to navigate home.

Panic seeped into my bones.

"Stay calm, stay focused," I told myself. My vision was "737 captain at London Heathrow," not "Tennessee crop duster (because I'd been kicked out of flight school)."

Focus on that.

Training kicked in. I pulled out my flashlight and slapped the map onto my lap. I dialed in the two radio beacons closest to my location. Where the two signals from each met, *that* should pinpoint my position—my fix.

It worked. From my position on the map, I plunked down a slide rule and drew a line to home base. Now all I had to do was follow that line home. I set heading.

The wind would try to drift me off course. I would correct.

Before long I heard familiar chatter on the home base radio. Then I saw the runway lights. And the airport beacon—winking at me against the sunset—guiding me home.

I called the base. And I started to breathe again.

"November 25503," crackled the base radio operator. "Cleared to land runway 35. Hey. Where you been all this time?"

"Cleared to land runway 35," I said, sweat dropping down my brow, rolling my jaw, hoping I'd dodged the question.

I squeaked the tires onto the runway, then opened the door to let the idling propeller blast sultry Memphis air into the cockpit.

Home.

But somehow, I thought as I taxied in, I was still lost.

Congratulations. If you followed all the steps, you have answered *The Question*. You are now *Self*-actualized and cleared for take-off.

Write down your vision. Say it:

Who are you?

Why are you here?

You just swore an oath. Commit!

That's how the true Self becomes your co-pilot. And it will always bring you home.

To your *true* home.

> *"I have learned to fly. Since then, I do not have to be pushed*
> *in order to move. Now I am nimble, now I fly, now I see myself*
> *under myself, now a god dances within me."*
> —Nietzsche

DAY **7**

WHO'S DRIVING?

A whale of a time

Follow-through defines trajectory.

Setting a course for "home" is one thing. But getting there is another thing entirely.

It's what happens *after* these seven days that will define the rest of our lives.

A famous story gives us an important piece of advice at this stage: Jonah and the Whale. God told Jonah: "Go to Nineveh. Speak the truth. Wake them up."

Jonah refused. He wasn't afraid of the people; he was afraid of the *mission*. He ran away, boarded a ship in the opposite direction, and tried to disappear.

But God-given purpose doesn't let go of us that easily.

The sea rose against him. A storm that wouldn't stop. The sailors begged for answers. Jonah knew. *This storm is because of me.*

He told them to throw him overboard. They did. The sea calmed.

Then the whale came and swallowed him. Three days in the belly of the whale, buried in darkness. Not dead, not alive. Just suspended.

This is a universal myth:

Those who refuse the call get swallowed by a beast of some kind—from whales to dragons—until they see the light.

The dark belly of the beast is the place of reflection and reckoning.

Jonah didn't slay the whale. He *surrendered* to it, to his destiny. And only then was he released. Spit back out, reborn.

This time, he obeyed.

He walked into Nineveh, spoke what needed to be spoken. The people listened. They changed. So did he.

That's why this condition is called the "Jonah Complex."

This is *not* the fear of failure.

Jonah Complex is the fear of what might happen if you say yes to the thing you were born to do.

We've all done it. After reading a personal development book, studying a course, or attending a seminar, most people drift. They'll feel an initial high, but will soon return to their baseline pattern:

- They slip back into the old ways—not consciously, but through small habits and familiar language.

- They confuse inspiration for action—they feel the high but build nothing upon it. They mistake clarity for completion—they think the decision was the work.

- They stay surrounded by people who mirror their previous mentality—and slowly back down from their vision.

- They remove all friction—no daily pressure, no visible cost for drift—until they wake up one day to find they're back in hell.

Not this time.

It's time to stop curating and start creating.

Now you are aligned with your true Self and the implicit purpose encoded within it. Your vision is now literally an expression of your biology. It's the high voltage charge lighting up your nervous system.

It is your calling and your *duty*.

But, as we touched on yesterday, as well as a true Self, we also have free will. And these two inner forces need to work together if we are to make our vision reality.

Seeing double

These two "selves" pulling in different directions is a major reason why most people fail to realize their vision.

It's like running in a three-legged race. If the two of you aren't synchronized, you'll trip up and never make it to the finish line.

So, let's get you both in sync.

We all feel this split to a certain degree, depending on how aligned these two selves are.

I recently had the honor of being invited to dinner with an indigenous Mi'kmaq tribe of northern Canada—the most gentle and sincere people I have ever met. When I asked one of the elders about this phenomenon, his answer didn't surprise me: "We believe we each have a young self and an old self in us. The old self is passed on. The young self will pass away at death. The young self must listen to the old self."

What the Mi'kmaq refer to as an "old self," we could refer to as the subconscious mind—because it's the ancient part of the psyche. It's collective, we all share it. This is where your Metageno type comes from. It's biological.

The "young self" could be referred to as consciousness— because it's the newest part of the psyche. It has grown out of the subconscious. It's unique to the individual. This is where your social mask (and hence self-report bias) come from. It's biographical.

And we need both.

(Note: This should *not* be confused with the Deleted Scene—a dissociated memory fragment that creates a temporary *sense* of duality. A Deleted Scene can surface, be integrated, and lose its power. That form of duality is resolvable. That is *not* the kind of duality being referred to here.)

Ancient culture and texts have been screaming about this phenomenon of human duality for thousands of years, as well as the necessity of curing this disorder by uniting the two selves:

- Ancient Egypt: The *ka* was understood as a kind of "second self"—a double that carried your life-force and stayed with you after death. In psychological terms, it represented the part of you that must remain connected to your core identity. Mummification was a ritual attempt to keep the self from splitting apart so it could be reborn whole. The fear wasn't having two selves—it was losing the thread that binds them. Integration meant continuity. Fragmentation meant oblivion.

- "Yoga" is derived from the Sanskrit word, "Yuj," which means *to yoke*, to bind together. Meditating and assuming certain positions in yoga classes are merely one of several means to that end of "binding together." Contrary to popular belief of many who attend yoga classes, the goal is not to "dissolve" or "destroy" ego, but rather to "yoke" it to the true Self.

- The Upanishads: "There are two selves... when one rises above I and me and mine, the Atman (the Godhead) is revealed as one's real Self." (Notice how the true Self is seen as the connection to God). And if there's one big takeaway from the Upanishads, it's this: "Wonderful is the one who speaks of the Self. Rare are they who make it the supreme goal of their lives...When the wise realize the Self... they go beyond sorrow."

- The Bhagavad Gita: "When your mind has overcome the confusion of duality, you will attain the state of holy indifference to things you hear and things you have heard."

- The Bible: "For I do not do the good I want, but the evil I do not want is what I keep on doing... I see in my members another law waging war against the law of my mind and making me captive to the law of sin."

- The Tao (paraphrased): "Only those who attain unity become what they are meant to be. If spirit (true Self) were not unified it would vanish."

Science eventually caught up with what ancients said about humans being split in two, and added interesting insights:

- In patients whose corpus callosum had been surgically cut to treat severe epilepsy—meaning the left and right brain could no longer communicate—researchers gave them a block design puzzle to solve with only their right hand. The right hand (controlled by left brain) struggled. Then something astonishing happened: the left hand (controlled by the right brain) reached over to help the right hand and solved the puzzle perfectly!

- Nobel prize-winning Daniel Kahneman explained the phenomenon as "System 1" and "System 2." His definition of System 1 matches that of the older, subconscious Self— it's instinctive, feeling, intuitive, fast, and comes from a deep source. It's "the older system," he explains, and "the secret author of many of the choices and judgments you make."

So, having dueling "voices" in your head doesn't make you insane.

It makes you human...

Dreams are messages from our psyche to "compensate"—to bring the two back in balance.

Those people you sometimes see going around talking to themselves are merely externalizing the inner drama we all share.

As our lives go on, the river of time forks. These two selves typically drift further apart, even though they're sharing the same space. In adulthood (usually after the age of 35 to 45) a civil war is raging inside us because of this, and we aren't sure which side is the right one—the side to trust and follow.

Division of these two selves leads to doubt, indecision, stress, and can even drive a person to mental breakdown.

Many of our ancient myths are cryptic messages to help us get our two selves synchronized. The Icarus myth is a perfect example, but it's often (and conveniently) misunderstood.

You probably know the tale...

Icarus and his father were given feathered wings so they could fly. And it worked.

But Icarus flew too close to the sun, and the wax that was keeping his feathers on started to melt from the heat.

His father yelled at him not to fly so close to the sun but Icarus didn't listen, and he fell to his death.

I don't believe this is a story that merely warns us about hubris (the common belief about this story).

It's about something much deeper:

1. Sun (and light) are symbols of the conscious mind ("Let there be light"). Icarus flew too close to it and paid the price. He was out of balance/sync.

2. A parental figure (his father) was present. Parents represent the Source of our existence, an ancient version—the true Self. Icarus was effectively not listening to the true Self.

We're now introducing more labels and descriptors for these two selves, so here is a recap and reference point for them all, integrating earlier ideas we discussed. Each column contains different names for the same thing (new terms in bold, categories and associations my own. *This table is symbolic, not literal*):

Biological	Biographical
True Self (Metageno Type)	Social Mask
Destiny	Free Will
"Old Self"	"Young Self"
System 1	System 2
Icarus's Dad	Icarus
Right brain	Left brain

Back to that naughty Icarus kid...

Icarus doesn't fail because he flies. He fails because he flies without having first integrated his true Self.

Aurelius explained: "Thou hast endured infinite troubles through not being contented with thy ruling faculty, when it does the things which it is constituted by *nature* to do."

"Flying" without integration of the true Self means missing out not only on purpose-alignment. It also means missing out on what could be regarded as a "special power..."

Have you ever got an amazing result from something you did *without thinking*?

You "just did it."

Maybe an amazing shot in a tennis game that stood out from your normal proficiency. Or something prophetic you said or wrote that seemed to come out of nowhere. Or throwing a roasted potato at a teacher's head with surreal accuracy...

Time distorted. It's as if it weren't you doing it.

And *afterwards*, as your *conscious* mind caught up with what just happened and tried to rationalize it, you realized that something instinctual and mystical seemed to have taken the wheel and nailed it. You weren't thinking, you weren't following a script... it just happened.

That's because you *weren't* thinking.

The true Self doesn't think. It acts. And when it does, *when we trust it and let go*, it shocks us with its ability.

It's the source of our "sixth sense." It's why we *instinctively know* people were talking about us as we enter a room. It's why we feel things in our *gut* (our body, not our head).

This is what we refer to as the "hidden hand." And ancient wisdom tries to show us how to find it and use it.

The Corpus Hermeticum said, "Pursue truth straight away, not according to preconceptions and fancies, but guided by the hand of *nature*."

The true Self is just one of our selves, though.

What about the other one?

The entity we want the true Self to be "yoked" to is consciousness.

Consciousness can also be called "*ego*-consciousness." We commonly abbreviate this to simply "ego" (and attach a negative label to it). On Day 3, we called the hero who saved the deleted scene our "director" or executive system. On Day 4, we saw how it can also create looping narratives if not managed (I also referred to it as "subjective consciousness" then—same thing). On Day 6, we revealed how the free will it gives us is a double-edged sword.

Let's update the mental map (new items in bold):

Subconscious	Ego-Consciousness
Biological	Biographical
True Self (Metageno Type)	Social Mask
Destiny	Free Will
"Old Self"	"Young Self"
System 1	System 2
Icarus's Dad	Icarus
Right brain	Left brain

Pop-spirituality talks about destroying, dissolving, or abandoning the ego. But this is not the true message.

The true message of what to do with ego is to cleanse it and master it. And that it must be united with the true Self.

To prove the point that we don't want to "kill" ego—that we *need* ego—look at the two drawings that follow (*eyeball it, DON'T measure it or overthink it!*) and *quickly* conclude—which of the two has the longest horizontal line?

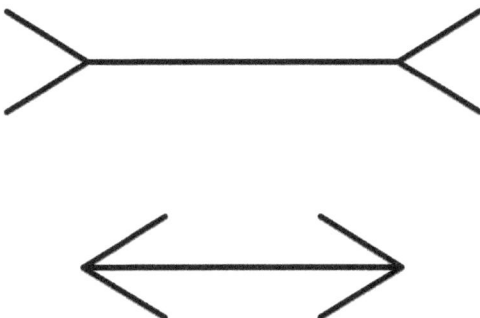

If you're like most people (*and* you followed my instructions), you quickly concluded that the top diagram has the longest horizontal line, right?

Wrong.

They're equal lengths.

It's called the Müller-Lyer illusion. Your fast, instinctual mind—left column of the map; System 1, and what I am referring to as the true Self—is the cause of you getting it wrong.

It "just did it."

And failed the test.

So, we need ego-consciousness—what I have placed on right column of the map; System 2—to figure certain things out. In short:

The two selves need each other. And we need them to need each other to realize our vision.

The trouble is that ego-consciousness, *unmanaged*, tends to get corrupted and arrogant, which is why we cleansed it in previous chapters. I believe this cleansing is what Nietzsche was referring to when he said, "Man is a polluted river. One must become a sea to receive a polluted river without becoming unclean."

Only when ego-consciousness is pure can it align with the true Self and start working for us instead of against us. And if it doesn't align? If it's not cleansed and brought to heel?

It runs the show. *And it throws you off course.*

It makes a scar-script your Vanishing Point, it makes you petrified of adversity, it sends you on fools' errands, and it doesn't give a damn about your true purpose... or your vision.

As Kahneman eloquently explains (parentheses and translations mine), "Although System 2 (ego) believes itself to be where the action is, the automatic System 1 (true Self) is the hero... System 2 (ego) would be a supporting character who believes herself to be the hero."

System 1 (true Self) knows what it wants: the purpose feels true and the signal is clear. But System 2 (ego) the executor, stalls. Kahneman showed that System 1 generates the impulse, while System 2 must "allocate attention to effortful activities" to act on it. When the two aren't synchronized, nothing moves.

In short, knowing who you are and why you're here isn't the challenge now. *Getting both systems to be true to your vision at the same time is.*

And that means:

- The tail needs to stop wagging the dog...

- Listening to Icarus's old man...

- Letting true Self be our captain, with ego-consciousness as its co-pilot.

How can we accomplish this?

Kahneman gave us a clue (parentheses and italics mine):

"If endorsed by System 2 (ego), impressions and intuitions (from the true Self) turn into *beliefs*."

And beliefs shape our reality.

So let's get System 2 to "endorse" our vision.

Hold your horses

Let's recap on our two selves that need integrating:

Subconscious	Ego-Consciousness
Biological	Biographical
True Self (Metageno Type)	Social Mask
Destiny	Free Will
"Old Self"	"Young Self"
System 1	System 2
Icarus's Dad	Icarus
Right brain	Left brain

And let's recap what we've said so far:

1. You discovered your Metageno type—what I am referring to as a representation of your true Self, the left side shown in the table...

2. From that discovery, you could see your purpose in life and created a vision for your life. We committed to an oath based on this...

3. However, since birth, a "second self" (or System 2) was slowly built over your true Self. Nurture and culture shaped your ego-consciousness, which resulted in your Deleted Scene...

4. As we grow older, tension ensues between the two selves, ultimately creating anxiety, depression, or something similar. To soothe the pain (we think) or to remain safe, ego creates and/or buys into numerous fantasies and becomes attached to them (explained in the Vanishing Point chapter).

5. So we cleanse ego of these contaminants...

6. And now, as the final step, we have agreed that ego needs to co-operate by "endorsing" our vision, which is an expression of the true Self...

And the key to accomplishing that final step is understanding this principle:

Ego is not the enemy. It's like a powerful horse that was running wild because of our neglect, pulling us in any direction that suited it.

So we tamed it...

And now we command it.

Harness it.

Blinker it.

And ride it home.

Never forgetting that it could throw us off at any time if we're not constantly and vigilantly maintaining control.

How can we accomplish this?

Let's first state how we will *not* accomplish it:

With what's been called "manifesting" and "affirmations."

"But!" some people may quickly react, "manifesting and affirmations absolutely work. Just the other day I chanted affirmations of abundance, and I closed a deal."

Great. Keep doing what's working (*if* you're 100% certain of the cause and effect). But I also see many people who feel disillusioned and saddened by the manifesting and affirmations narrative because they were sold a big lie that goes something like this:

Dear Santa,

I have been a good boy this year. Please can I have:

Insert wish list here—typically all the materialistic shit you think you want.

Thank you!

They stick this note on the fridge and just wait. They make no effort. They feel no sense of accountability. And yet they're surprised when nothing happens.

I am *not* saying you can't have anything you want. I'm saying that the methodology and/or explanation being used by many people to get it is wrong.

"But it's now scientifically proven!" people might say, citing quantum physics and language like "collapse of the wave function," etc. Fine, let's look at that.

The thinking goes like this:

"At the subatomic level, everything is vibrating particles (true). And when these particles are observed, they "collapse" into reality (true).

Therefore, if a human "vibrates" at the same frequency as that which is desired, we "attract" that which is desired."

Last part *sounds* true, right? There's just one problem with it:

That's not how quantum physics works.

I'm not saying science has all the answers. Not at all. What I'm saying is that *if we're going to quote quantum physics for something*, perhaps it's only fair that we hear what quantum physics has to say about all this. I imagine a quantum physicist would say this:

- In quantum experiments, the "observer" isn't some guy with a vision board and a latte. It's a machine. A cold, dead instrument. A photon detector. A particle counter. Not "Karen's affirmations of a Range Rover."

- Quantum mechanics applies to subatomic particles in sealed labs—electrons, quarks, photons. Not your twin flame. Not your crypto portfolio.

- You wouldn't cite thermodynamics to explain why your ex ghosted you, so don't quote quantum physics to justify manifesting a second home in Aspen.

"Okay, okay, but what's the harm in manifesting and affirmations?"

Umm...

Turns out, *affirmations can actually backfire*, especially if you don't believe them...

Wood, Perunovic & Lee (2009), clinical study: Participants with low self-esteem were told to repeat things like "I am lovable." The result? They felt *worse*. Why? Because their subconscious called bullshit to what ego was trying to convince itself of.

When your internal reality doesn't match the words coming out of your mouth, your brain doesn't go, "Oh wow, what a lovely reframe." It goes: "Liar!"

That's called cognitive dissonance, and your nervous system hates it. It enters a stress state, reinforcing the opposite of the affirmation.

You can chant, "I'm wealthy," but your gut responds: "Bro, you just overdrew on a coffee."

Oettingen et al. (2009) clinical study: Fantasizing about success (without action) actually lowers energy and follow-through. Why? Because the brain thinks you've already succeeded. It checks the box. Mission accomplished. Meanwhile, you're still living with your parents.

In short: If you *pretend* to be someone you're not, your subconscious true Self *knows.*

This idea about "tricking" the subconscious (the "Old Self") into believing this or that is akin to an infant believing it's pranking an adult when the ruse is painfully obvious, even quaint.

So what *is* the truth? Is there a jewel in the mud of misinformation?

Yes.

Narrate this

There *is* a kind of "magic" in play...

A simple demonstration will explain. Let's say that today you decide you're going to buy a Ford Escort. What happens over the next few days?

You suddenly and "mysteriously" start to see more Ford Escorts on the road.

They seem to be everywhere.

It feels weird. Like reality is responding.

But has the number of Ford Escorts on the road suddenly increased since you made the decision to buy one?

Did you "manifest" them?

Did chanting "I want a Ford Escort!" attract them?

Of course not.

So, what happened?

What feels like "attraction" is actually perception filtering via something called the Reticular Activating System, or RAS.

The RAS is like the reins on a horse. It's what we steer our lives towards. Or not.

Here's how it works. For survival, ancient humans evolved a data filtering and targeting system that we can harness today.

When you *persistently* lock onto a vision, the RAS starts filtering for data that supports your vision.

And there's the catch:

The ancient RAS doesn't check for truth. *It only checks for relevance to your persistent vision.*

It doesn't know what's "real," it knows what's been repeated, emotionally charged, or tagged as important by you.

Which is why what you mentally tag as important should be *aligned with what you want*. And not what you don't want, like that looping scar-script we burned on Day 4.

In summary:

It's not "fake it till you make it."

It's "forge it until it fits."

This is what the process called "visualization" *truly* is.

Visualization is *rehearsing a believable, earned future.* Mentally rehearse your type-based vision, *every day*, until it becomes reality.

This is the type-specific canyon we gallop through, with ego as the horse, the RAS as the reins, and true Self as the rider.

So before we ride off into the sunset, let's learn how to ride.

Ride or die

Let's now look at the whole process of type-specific visualization.

These are what I refer to as the nine gates of visualization. Each gate you pass through refines what your RAS locks onto, until it can't help but steer you toward the inevitable:

ONE: Make your vision type-specific

We've already done this in the previous chapter, but I have more to say about it.

Knowing your Metageno type and making your vision a direct expression of it is your masterstroke game-changer. Why? Because:

You don't need to pretend to be what you already are.

Type F3 "Vedana" already *is* a spiritual leader, Type M3 "Kalo" already *is* a creative artist, even if they didn't previously realize this. And the equivalent applies to all the types.

It's birthright, not bullshit.

Your mind won't call "liar!" if you play out what you were always meant to be, even if the vision for it isn't fully realized yet.

Seeing your type = Activating your type = RAS filters reality to match.

And:

When your vision is aligned with your true Self, motivation is automatic and effortless.

Because your vision came, as Maslow would put it, "out of one's real Self rather than out of the idealized pseudo-self."

When you are "pulled," you don't need to "push."

By the same principle, you don't have to try hard to be your Self and simply realize the destiny that was evidently encoded in your genes.

We don't fake success; we keep pushing forward, saying, "This is who I am and always was. And anything less feels foreign."

TWO: Tame and train the "horse"

I compared ego to a powerful horse that was running wild due to our neglect as its handler. When our "horse" was running amok, thinking it was in charge, it told RAS to allow random and undesirable elements into our minds.

So we "tamed and trained" this horse in the previous chapters.

Now we ride this horse to our vision, blinkered and on a tight rein. And we need to *keep* it on a tight rein...

The horse will try to look back at where you've been...

Pull the reins forward.

The horse will try to veer off the path, tempted by distractions...

Pull the reins back on track.

The horse will try to stop...

Nudge your spurs into it, keep moving.

The horse will try to throw you off...

Let it know who the master is, stay on it.

As you ride, constantly ask yourself: "Is what I am about to do/say/ think keeping me on course or off course to my vision?"

If the answer is "no," then correct course.

THREE: Blinkers, not blinders

Our vision must be within the realm of possibility. To make a silly example to prove the point, we can't successfully visualize ourselves sprouting wings and flying (Icarus was just a story: do not attempt at home).

This point may sound obvious until you realize how often people try to visualize something that isn't real. Relationships are a great example of this...

Many people searching for romance create a wish-list of Mr./Mrs. Perfect. Of course, such a person doesn't exist unless you're dating a spreadsheet.

Now you have Metageno type awareness, you know this. All fourteen types are laid bare, their strengths and weaknesses, *their true Self.* That's how they come, it's how they were born. No "I'll change them," or "He'll change... he's a fixer-upper." The relationship graveyard is packed with tombstones that read: "I thought they would change." You can't visualize your way into a relationship with a unicorn. Especially if the unicorn doesn't like being told to change.

And have any of those lonely hearts created any closet space for their new life-partner? No. But there's still half a wardrobe devoted to their ex's hoodie "just in case."

To *real*-ize a vision the vision has to be real, heartfelt, and not half-assed.

FOUR: Love it or leave it

Without emotion, there is no ignition.

You can sit around all day thinking lofty thoughts, but if there's no fire underneath them, your nervous system doesn't care.

And this isn't poetic, it's biological...

A thought without emotion is neurologically irrelevant. But when it's fused with high-arousal feeling—rage, awe, hunger, desire—it sets off a biochemical chain reaction (the amygdala and hippocampus lock in, and neuromodulators like norepinephrine and cortisol flood the system — McGaugh, 2004; Cahill & McGaugh, 1998).

Suddenly, that thought isn't just noise, it's a directive.

Emotion is the fuse.

This should already be covered by your vision being type-aligned, but you need to also feel the emotions behind it.

Tip: create a playlist of songs that fire you up and help you feel the emotions of your vision—music hits us at the deepest level.

FIVE: Mental rehearsal (the good kind)

Here is where the rubber hits the road (or where the horseshoes hit the dirt), and we reap the rewards of the work we did training the "horse" back in the Vanishing Point chapter...

Recall how an untrained ego-consciousness (or subjective consciousness) creates unproductive (and often untrue) stories that keep us locked in the past, usually creating a self-pity loop and false identity. In effect, our mind was mentally rehearsing the things we didn't want, in full detail and high definition.

Now, the exact same way, we reverse that process and mentally rehearse what we *do* want. Tell a new story, control the internal narrative.

Many people say they struggle to visualize. Admittedly, some Metageno types naturally find it easier than others. But I have noticed that the same people who say they struggle to visualize have no problem when it comes to visualizing their nightmare scenario in all its gory detail!

That's the horse controlling the rider.

Get a grip. Literally.

Bonus: When your mind is *fully* occupied with your vision it doesn't have time to feel sorry for itself or dwell on past failures.

Here's the deal. When you visualize with intensity and realism, your brain can't tell the difference between reality and imagined reality. MRI studies show that visualizing an action activates the same neural circuits as doing it.

Your brain can't distinguish between real action and vividly imagined action.

Elite athletes, performers, and entrepreneurs all use visualization— not because it bends reality, but because it programs the mind to expect and train for the outcome.

This isn't tricking the brain, it's training it. When you visualize something accurately, you are priming neural circuits for that behavior. This reduces hesitation, tightens motor response, and increases follow through.

It's like a memory that hasn't happened yet. See it. Feel it. Smell it. Every tiny detail.

"How about vision boards?" I'm often asked. If vision boards help you visualize, great, just remember they're simply that: a visual aid that doesn't do the work for you.

SIX: Ride like the wind

Imagine you've become the world's greatest visualizer. Perfect focus. Crystal clarity. Emotional charge at full throttle.

Then I lock you in a prison cell and throw away the key.

Will your vision become reality?

Of course not.

Because nothing moves without action.

You can see it. Feel it. Rehearse it down to the pores in your skin. But unless your body moves, your reality won't.

Here's the actual cycle:

True Self powered vision = visualization = thoughts

= ACTIONS

= habits = reality = results = feedback =
continued actions = self-fulfilling loop

The nervous system is wired for it. But it only kicks into gear when you stop simulating and start doing. Most people manage the attention part. But they never follow through with intention.

They visualize, but don't ride. The horse just merrily grazes in the field.

They wish, beg, chant affirmations, wait. Hoping the horse rides itself. But here's what really happens when you act:

Even a small action—sending the email, booking the call, hitting the gym—triggers dopamine. That dopamine reinforces the neural pathway: "This matters. Do more."

You feel momentum. You feel capable. The horse starts moving because now it has direction.

It's that point when we're on a diet when, after weeks of nothing happening, we get on the scales one day and, finally, we see we're losing weight. Now we're motivated to continue.

Without action, that positive loop dies on the launchpad. Your brain thinks it's all just a fantasy. And no matter how type-specific and vivid the vision is, if you don't move?

It's dead on arrival.

SEVEN: Jump the obstacles

There is no such thing as a barrier—only a barrier for a particular person trying to get what they want.

Most people visualize the dream. Elite performers also visualize the potential chaos.

They don't just see the perfect outcome; they mentally walk through everything that could go wrong. Every setback. Every sabotage. Every detour. Why?

So they don't flinch *when* it happens. So their nervous system isn't caught off guard.

They've already been there. It's all part of the mental rehearsal.

It's called implementation intention—a method proven to increase follow-through and resilience by mentally rehearsing potential obstacles *and* the response to them. Not just the path, but the potholes.

But here's the paradox:

You must see the obstacle *without giving it energy*. You don't dwell on it. You pre-load the response. Then you move on.

You don't visualize failure to entertain it. You visualize it to disarm it. Like a rider anticipating a horse's buck, you stay ready, legs tight, reins firm, vision forward. The obstacle comes. You've already jumped it in your mind. Now you just follow through.

EIGHT: One mile at a time

I love big, audacious visions. But they can come at a price, and I don't just mean from the work involved.

A big vision, or a vision that you don't yet feel worthy or capable of, can be intimidating. It can provoke mental resistance, and that's a problem for accurate visualization and RAS. So we need a method to tackle this challenge.

The next time you walk up a flight of stairs—something you usually do without thinking—try this experiment:

Climb the stairs, looking down at the previous step you took as you go.

You probably stumbled. Try again. This time look down at your feet as you go.

Better, but still not comfortable. Next, try looking at the top of the staircase, where you *ultimately* want to be.

Better, but still a little awkward, no? Next, climb the stairs as normal, and pay attention to where your eyes naturally go...

You look at the next few steps you're about to make. Not the top stair. Not the current stair. Not the stair behind you.

Translated into our purposes:

If your vision is big, break it down into all the required steps to get you from A to B.

Then visualize accomplishing only the next steps ahead of you.

Never lose sight of the big vision—the steps are the means to that end—it's okay and even natural to visualize one step at a time.

This is how you "magically" wake up one day to find your vision became a reality.

And here's the funny part if you've been doing it right...

When that great day comes, it will seem like an anticlimax. Why? Because by then you'll have seen your vision so many times in your head that when reality finally catches up, you'll say to yourself, "Well, duh." That bottle of champagne you were saving for when the great day came? Whatever.

NINE: Get out of the way of your Self

The final and ninth gate of visualization deserves special attention because it's the part that gets most overlooked, the part that somehow activates the other 8 gates. And because it's as mysterious as it is powerful, simple, and instantly relatable to experience.

Somehow, we all know the story of a couple who can't conceive a child. So, they adopt one, and then they suddenly *do* conceive, right on cue.

What happened?

We can explain *some* of this phenomenon, but not all of it. Let's take a look at what this couple did *or didn't do* to get what they wanted.

Most of the previous gates also come together in this case study:

A. They stopped stressing.
Their white-knuckled grip on "I *must* get pregnant" let go.

B. They retained the vision.
They didn't stop wanting to conceive a child of their own. They didn't give up; they *surrendered*—there's a difference, as we said on Day 2.

C. They visualized being parents 24/7.
They were living it. They weren't tricking their minds; they were training them. The stroller and the diapers were already there because they now knew a baby was coming.

D. They took action.
They had sex. Phone sex won't cut it.

E. They were no longer attached to the outcome of their efforts.
Ah. This is the big master stroke for the proverbial childless couple who adopt. And this is the ninth gate:

Non-attachment to the outcome of your actions.

It's enjoying the ride. It's letting go of the outcome. Giving it all you've got... and then letting it go...

It's making your love (of the act) unconditional.

Which is another reason why your vision should stem from your true Self; it makes your love of the act unconditional.

But when you fixate on the outcome of your actions in the present, you trigger stress and doubt. Execution gets sloppy. You begin to react to lack rather than move from alignment.

The RAS will lock onto *what's missing*, not what you're moving toward.

That's why ancient wisdom says (emphasis mine):

Bhagavad Gita: "Those who are motivated only by desire for the fruits of action are miserable, for they are constantly anxious about the results of what they do. When *consciousness is unified*, however, all vain anxiety is left behind."

Tao: "They are not focused on outcomes or achievements; therefore, they always succeed... Over-concern is just as harmful as disregard."

Or, as music legend Charlie Parker put it, "Master the instrument, master the music, then forget all that shit and play."

The harder you "try," the more you reinforce that you don't have it yet. If you chase something desperately, your energy is needy, anxious, and uncertain. But when you are calmly certain, things happen.

It's not that you stop wanting, it's that you stop doubting.

This phenomenon is not anecdotal. It appears across cultures, eras, and fields of study, showing up in psychology, anthropology, creativity research, and spiritual literature. Different disciplines describe it differently, but they describe the same pattern.

Science can't fully explain this. And why the breakthrough happens *when* it does—remains a total mystery.

Deus ex machina

Going down...!

Two minutes to live...!

Ugh! I jolted awake in my bed, lurching my body upward, clutching my chest, and gasping for air as if my head had been held underwater.

I glanced at the digital clock at my bedside. Sunday, 3:12 a.m., about three hours before the alarm, when I'd need to get up and get ready to head to the airport for my flight home to Miami.

I dropped back onto the bed. As I hit the pillow, a realization barged into my head: that wasn't a nightmare I'd just had.

It was a memory.

And, for the first time since that day, I let it play out in full...

1993. I was running out of money and immigration visa time, and I couldn't return to England without 700 total hours. This was needed to convert the American pilot license to a British one, or the whole exercise would've been a waste of time.

So, after earning my American Commercial Pilot License, I decided to get away from Memphis and drive down to Miami in search of work.

With what savings I had left, I found a shabby apartment to share with two other starving pilots (and half the entire cockroach population of Florida).

Then I went job hunting. In early 1993, airlines were still licking their wounds from a nasty recession.

Hurricane Andrew blasting through the region the previous October hadn't helped.

My luck changed when a small air taxi and freight outfit didn't slam the door in my face. Perhaps leading my pitch with "I'll fly for free" did the trick. My only hope was that I'd reach 700 hours before I went broke.

So, I flew twin-engine Cessna 402 aircraft out of Miami International Airport into the Bahamas and Caribbean, slicing the sticky air over crystal water known as the Bermuda Triangle (a.k.a. "The Devil's Triangle").

It was easy to see why The Devil's Triangle had earned its name, and why so many vessels had been lost there or had reported strange sightings. The islands all looked alike from the air, the weather could be as stealthy as it was violent, and if you miss your visual cues and fly past your destination, all that lies ahead is an empty dark ocean.

I was flying a much bigger aircraft now, but it was still relatively small, and the tropical weather could be a challenge. Sometimes thunderstorms were cloaked by larger cloud formations, and, without weather radar, you couldn't see them.

Flying between layers of cloud presented the most insidious and deadly of optical illusions if a pilot didn't learn to trust the aircraft's instruments. Mistakenly using a cloud layer as your visual reference of the horizon meant the aircraft could enter a gradual, but unnoticeable, roll which, if not checked, would lead to a spinning dive.

Back at Miami, I became a revered curiosity in the all-Hispanic neighborhood I was living in, near Hialeah. A few people asked if I'd fly no-questions-asked packages for them but apart from that, I was welcomed by my "nuevos amigos" and cared for by a Colombian girlfriend (neither one of us spoke a word of the other's language, but it seemed to work).

Thankfully, they all kept me fed with empanadas and guava rolls. The only catch was they demanded to hear me tell stories about Big Ben. Fine. But there are only so many stories you can make up about a clock, and as I wrote letters to my grandparents on the front porch I felt a growing pang of homesickness in my stomach. I watched the British Airways 747 launch into amber sky each evening, outbound for London. I didn't just want to be on it; I wanted to be flying it.

I wasn't just counting flight hours; I was scribbling them in my logbook, each entry taking me closer to home.

I was only a few weeks from finally flying home to London when it happened.

My weather radar wasn't working that day, but it wasn't a legal requirement to have it, and if I didn't go, I'd probably have lost the job. I just needed to do my time and get home.

So I took off, anyway.

The sky was white, wet, and stormy as I lifted off the runway, but nothing I hadn't seen before. I was soon flying through cloud, merrily flying by instruments, carrying cargo to Nassau.

About ten minutes later, the sky suddenly turned dark, as if the lights had turned out.

The bumps began, disturbingly more violent than usual.

Heavy rain lashed the windshield.

Then the hail came, hard and thick, against the fuselage—like a machine gun trying to shoot me down, rat-a-tat. The sound of the ice hitting the windshield was so loud I thought it might break.

I called Miami Center for a heading out of the storm.

But the hail was so loud I couldn't hear a reply.

Then the storm took control of my aircraft. I was being thrown about like a toy, brutally humbled by the elements.

And I was losing altitude.

The aircraft had become locked in a powerful downdraft that sent it into an involuntary descent. My instruments showed a descent rate of 3,000 feet per minute.

I was only at 6,000 feet, so that gave me about two minutes to live, I remember telling myself.

I applied full power and tried to climb.

The engines screamed.

Lightning flashed.

I couldn't pull up.

Going down...!

Two minutes to live...!

Training kicked in: I watched my instruments, trying to keep the wings level, hoping it would be over soon.

But the Atlantic Ocean was getting closer.

The horror of potentially ditching in the water stung my gut. Terror gripped my spine. I snatched the life jacket out from under my seat. I couldn't tell if it was sweat or tears I tasted. I tuned the second radio to 121.5—the emergency channel in preparation for the mayday call.

This is it.

That's when I heard what I could only describe as an "inner voice" *commanding* me—to act against my training of only looking down at my instruments.

It clearly said: *"Look up. Look up!"*

Wincing with confusion, I complied. I peeked over the instrument panel, briefly scanning my field of vision through the windshield...

Then I saw it, to my right, slightly lower: a shaft of light in the darkness. A translucent hole in the storm. *A way through.*

The brick in my stomach dissolved into ecstasy. I steered toward the light. I wasn't flying; I was reaching out with every fiber in my body.

Wisps of cloud raced past me, gradually thinning out, teasing me into the light.

I punched through to the clear sky on the other side of the storm, engines still screaming. And closer to the ocean than I wanted to acknowledge.

I pretended it hadn't happened. Shut out the shame.

And the salvation.

The day of relief finally came: 700 hours in the logbook. The twin propellers of my weatherworn Cessna 402 rocked to a halt for the last time. I was going home.

Years later, the buried memory of this near death experience had woken me up. I couldn't go back to sleep. I lay in bed, alone in the dark, and contemplated this event.

"Sometimes illumination comes to our rescue at the very moment when all seems lost; we have knocked at every door and they open on nothing until, at last, we stumble unconsciously against the only one through which we can enter the kingdom we have sought in vain a hundred years—and it opens." – Proust.

It's as if there's a test we have to pass if we want to get somewhere. A persistence test. A test to see how much adversity we can suffer before we give up. And often, it's right at that point when we're about to let go that we break through.

Science can see where the brain lights up when this long-documented "Inner Voice" shows up, but it can't explain *why* it shows up in the nick of time.

We've arrived at a mystical frontier.

The phenomenon of this "Inner Voice" reaches far back into human history—in fact, it evidently *shaped* it. We used to believe it was the voice of God—many of us still do. Joan of Arc's story—a freedom fighter driven by an Inner Voice—is one of many such tales. The human experience is littered with them.

Ancient texts tell us to get out of the way of the Inner Voice. Taking the Bible as just one example, from lines like "Be still, and know that I am God" to the story of Elijah when he heard the "still small voice..."

Elijah was burned out and running for his life when he climbed a mountain to hear from God. A raging wind came, but God wasn't in it. Then an earthquake. Still no God. Then fire. Still nothing. Only afterward, in the silence, came what the text calls a "still small voice." That's where the Divine showed up.

Being silent was partly what Day 2 was about. To literally "hear our-*selves* think."

It may be a "still, small voice," but, paradoxically, it also has a kind of parental authority to it. Like Icarus's dad.

Indeed, the entire Corpus Hermeticum is an account of a deity (Poemander) portrayed as a "father" speaking to his "son." Poemander said "I know what you wish, and I am always present with you."

This idea of God as parent is echoed in the heart of Greek mythology. Notice how all the Greek heroes like Perseus were the offspring of a God but raised by human stepparents (superhero stories like Superman also follow this myth). The word "enthusiasm" is derived from the Greek word "entheos," which translates as "to be filled with a god."

I believe this is also where the concept of a "Godparent" comes from. In Latin (patrinus/matrina) godmother/godfather literally means "*little* father/mother." Symbolically, it is a spiritual parent, or soul-sponsor—an entity responsible for your spiritual path.

We speak of having a "*God*-given" purpose, of doing "God's work." And the common phrase in Arabic: "Inshallah" (if God wills it).

These stories and beliefs are all trying to articulate a kind of divinity within us, that *is* us, and yet paradoxically *not* us:

- The Bhagavad Gita shows God saying, "I am come to life in them." The Upanishads talk of a "thumb-sized being enshrined in the heart." The deeper translation of the Hindu greeting "Namaste" is "The Divine *within* me bows to the Divine *in* you."

- Marcus Aurelius made continual reference to "the deity within," and said, "Every man's intelligence is a god, and is an efflux of the deity... Look within. Within is the fountain of good, and it will ever bubble up, if thou wilt ever dig."

- Islam speaks of the *ruh* (divine breath) and *fitrah* (innate nature): a built-in spark of God *within—quiet, guiding, and always pulling us back to truth.*

- "Behind your thoughts and feelings stands a mighty commander—an unknown sage," said Nietzsche.

- Jung spoke of "the Great Man within."

But I think one of the best explanations of this and the associated paradox comes from anthropologist Levy-Bruhl when he relayed the Aborigine belief of a person's "Iningukua:"

"The iningukua accompanies him throughout life, warns him of the dangers threatening him and helps him to escape from them. He is a sort of deity or guardian angel..."

And regarding the paradox of it being us and yet *not* being us:

"But ought we to say perhaps, since the individual and his iningukua are but one, he is himself his own guardian? No doubt in one aspect,

the individual is the iningukua. But from another point of view, this iningukua is distinct from him."

And regarding its immortal and divine nature Levy-Bruhl continued, echoing the mentality behind Egyptian mummification and the desire to ensure the *ka* remains with the body:

"It lived before him and will not die with him."

A "guardian angel." Interesting that the word "God" traces back to the Proto-Indo-European root "Gheu" which translates as "The one called upon."

There must be some reason why the 14 Metageno type characters keep regenerating in humans. Perhaps Heraclitus explained when he said, "A man's character is his guardian divinity."

The word "religion" comes from the Latin "religio" which means "to bind *back*." This suggests a reversion to something that we already had but became disconnected from. Could this disconnection be from the Inner Voice?

Religion, in its original form, may have been an attempt to bind us back to that voice, but over time, it replaced the voice with rules.

All great religions, at their core, cite the same truth: the Divine isn't out there—it's within. The deeper thread across Christianity, Hinduism, Islam, Buddhism, and more is this:

You already have direct access.

But somewhere along the way we missed this alignment. We stopped hearing the Voice, and started narrating instead, as explained in the Vanishing Point chapter.

So, the Voice didn't die. We just got too loud to hear it, unless in crisis *or* in flow with our purpose in life. As Maslow said, we are "most unified in integration when successfully facing either a great joy or creative moment or else a major problem or a threat or emergency."

This is echoed by Jung and his protégé, Neumann:

Jung: "The ego's discursive flow of representations (which goes from one thought to another) and its desires (which run from one object to another) calm down when the Great Man within is encountered."

Neumann: "The 'voice,' the utterances of the Self, will never speak in a disintegrated personality."

A skeptic might argue that this Inner Voice is some kind of hallucination, a glitch, or an ancient survival artifact. But if that's true, why does it sound like duty, not delusion? Why does it often carry a sense of rightness, even destiny?

The Inner Voice is a *subjective* experience. The subjective experience —the feeling of being *you*—cannot be measured by science, yet we know it exists.

And science can't explain the fortuitous *timing* of the Inner Voice's commands. It *can* say that it appears to come from the right brain. (Sidebar: Remember how in the split brain experiments I mentioned earlier, the left hand came to the rescue of the right hand to solve the puzzle? The *right brain* controls the left hand. Also interesting: the vanishing point in Da Vinci's famous *Last Supper* painting is not the center of Christ's face as you'd expect—it's located on his *right* temple.)

Since we learned to fly—not much more than only a century ago— we unconsciously unraveled a primordial belief that existed perhaps for as long as humans gazed at the stars: *our gods exist in the sky*. We walked where gods were supposed to walk and we didn't see them up there. This silent and subtle yet seismic shock to the system left us spiritually disoriented.

But perhaps the gods never were in the sky, and we're only now revisiting the idea that the "gods" are within us.

Andrew Carnegie, the Scottish-American industrialist, was one of the richest men of his time. He said the secret to his success was what he called the "Other Self." He offered insight on how we might benefit from it:

"I do not know what this other self is, but I do know that there can be no permanent defeat for the man or woman who discovers it and relies upon it. It follows no precedents, recognizes no limits, and always finds a way to accomplish desired ends. It may meet with temporary defeat, but not with permanent failure..."

"... It is a force so intangible in nature that the majority of men never recognize it... Noteworthy is the fact that this other self seldom exerts its influence or makes itself known excepting at times of unusual emergency, when men are forced, through adversity and temporary defeat, to change their habits and to think their way out of difficulty."

But he cautions, if we are to use it successfully:

"Our other self will not do your work for you; it will only guide you intelligently in achieving for yourself the objects of your desires... *Keep doubt and fear and worry entirely out of your mind.*"

That last sentence is another reason to see subjective (ego) consciousness—that internal noise-maker we discussed on Day 4 and 5—for what it is: a potential *problem*.

Let's update our map (new additions in bold):

Subconscious ————————	Ego-Consciousness
Biological ————————	Biographical
True Self ———————— (Metageno Type)	Social Mask
Destiny ————————	Free Will
"Old Self" ————————	"Young Self"
System 1 ————————	System 2
Icarus's Dad ————————	Icarus
Right brain ————————	Left brain
Inner Voice ————————	**Internal Noise**

Is this two-sided mental map a signpost not just for individuals, but for the human species?

Let's ask F. Scott Fitzgerald:

"The test of a first-rate intelligence is the ability to hold two opposed ideas in the mind at the same time and still retain the ability to function."

Looking around today, I think it might be an understatement to say we're struggling to prove ourselves as a "first-rate intelligence." Perhaps an alien species would agree.

"Them and us" thinking comes from primitive tribal thinking.

Subjective consciousness turns that into ideologies.

Ideologies replace curiosity with dogma.

Dogma draws the curtain and calls the darkness truth.

The tiresome tug of war—both inside and outside us—is a projection of the human collective, which is a projection of the individual.

Take myths, stories, and scripture as an example. They are loaded with encoded wisdom that teaches us how to live and how to move forward. Learning from them and retaining them is conservative. Writing the next chapters is progressive. Humans must do both to evolve.

It's possible to be conservative and progressive at the same time.

This is what it means to "hold two opposed ideas in the mind at the same time and still retain the ability to function." *This is what it means to evolve.*

Ego-consciousness taking the lead role was once necessary—to pull away from the darkness of our animal origins. But that was only a steppingstone in our evolution.

The next step is not "more thinking." It's less narration and more direct experience. It's not the end of consciousness; it's the end of self-commentary as the dominant mode.

Presence and pure perception must replace commentary and confabulation.

The Inner Voice and the Hidden Hand *are not conscious.* They completely bypass subjective consciousness and the counterproductive narrative it can generate.

If human evolution continues toward states of constant flow, we are not losing consciousness—we are losing the narrator that interrupts it...

To exist in an almost permanent state of flow.

Could that be possible?

There's only one way to find out. But it certainly will be impossible if we don't silence the inner narrator of subjective consciousness.

We aren't born with subjective consciousness, so why can't we unlearn it? It's not until around age 6 that we *acquire* it.

If someone cuts us off on the road we invent a story about why they did it and what it means ("Mother *fucker*! What, does he think he's better than me, or something?). Meanwhile, the three-year-old princess watching the same event from her car seat just thinks "dangerous driver" and goes back to her coloring book.

Maybe kids are here to teach *us*, rather than the other way around.

When we integrate the two halves to become a whole we will pass through the next gate.

Spirituality versus science is a schism that must be urgently resolved.

Spirituality rejecting science denies us the future. And science denying spirituality denies us the full human experience. We cannot afford to reject half of what we are. As we said on Day 5: nature abhors a vacuum, *fear adores a vacuum.*

Perhaps the search never ends or is never meant to end. Perhaps the search itself is the point—and we aren't meant to know.

As one of the most famous scientists of all time—Albert Einstein—said: "The most beautiful thing we can experience is the mysterious. It is the source of all art and science."

It's not about choosing a side. It's about joining the sides to create the whole.

Icarus must reunite with his father if we are to fly into our future.

So let's light our final match...

Burn the map to reforge it into something new *and whole,* and let's write our third act—and humanity's—at the same time.

Subconscious	Ego-Consciousness
Biological	Biographical
True Self (Metageno Type)	Social Mask
Destiny	Free Will
"Old Self"	"Young Self"
System 1	System 2
Icarus's Dad	Icarus
Right brain	Left brain
Inner Voice	Internal Noise
Spirituality	**Science**

There's evidently something in you that is not merely human. Forgotten, maybe, but not gone. The only thing that can never be taken from you. The part of you that looks on, goes on, and helps reforge something stronger from the broken pieces of a former life.

So you are not alone on your journey.

You never were. And you never will be.

Remember this after these seven days, as you visualize what you now know you were put here to do. And as you face adversity, now, and hereafter.

Between you and your destination there will be storms you can't avoid. But somewhere in that darkness is the light you were destined to follow.

Find it. Trust it.

And follow it to the other side of the squall, where the air is so clear you could cry at its purity.

No *sub*-mission.

No ending.

Fly for the light

I leapt out of bed. I paced around the room. Then I did something for the first time in my life: I kneeled and gave thanks. I didn't know what or who I was thanking, all I felt was deep gratitude. For my life. For the day the heavens chewed me up and spat me out. For the duty I was now charged with.

It's hard to explain how the breakthrough felt. It was like I was no longer trying to save a sinking ship—I had burned the ship and become the ocean.

For each day this week, I had written a single line as a kind of take-away poem—something to ensure the lessons of each day weren't lost. Now I wrote the seventh line as the start of a new verse:

Day 1: *Darkness makes sparks of hope burn bright,*
Day 2: *Turning ash to stars that forge new light.*
Day 3: *Through flame, the shadows turn to gold,*
Day 4: *Freedom's the treasure no scar sold.*
Day 5: *We stand unblinking where death takes aim,*
Day 6: *And fix our sight on the world we claim.*
Day 7: *Beyond the edge of knowing, the Self unfolds,*

Later, as I was completing my packing, the front doorbell rang.

My mother had forgotten her key. I opened the front door and let her in from the cold. It was time for her to deliver me to the airport.

"You're only halfway through your photo album," she said, holding it up at the 1993 pages. "What about the rest?"

"Some other time," I said, smiling. "Let's go."

"What about breakfast?"

"There's a diner at Heathrow that serves pancakes. I'll get breakfast there."

As I walked out the door, I paused to gaze at the blackthorn blossoms that had sprung to life.

We were soon driving east on the A303 road, passing Stonehenge as David Bowie sang *Starman* on the *Hits from the 70s!* radio station. I slid my sunglasses on to meet the rising sun, then glanced around at the car and smiled. 1977 all over again—my mother driving me to school. To meet with The Wizard.

"How do you feel?" she said anxiously.

"Like a racehorse at the starting gate!"

She smiled through tears of relief.

I stared out at the road ahead. I wasn't flying home, nor was I leaving home. Heart is where the home is.

I wanted another audience with The Wizard. I had unanswered questions.

And I had a new drawing to show him.

Thanks for spending the week with me!

If you enjoyed the book, I would be so
grateful for your review.

Go to **www.Burnin.Love** or scan below
to be taken directly to the Amazon page:

About the author

James Sheridan is an award-winning and international bestselling author, a CPD-certified and published psychology researcher, and the founder of the Sheridan-Metageno® Personality Test (SMPT). He was awarded the title of Coach of Excellence in recognition of his work with individuals and organizations, and is a public speaker and business consultant to clients that have included NASDAQ-listed corporations. Originally from London, England, Sheridan rose from humble beginnings to build a remarkable and eclectic career that has included professional ice hockey, commercial aviation as a jet captain, and setting a world airspeed record in experimental aircraft. His previous titles span multiple genres and include *The You Code*, *Kiss Fewer Frogs*, and *The Pandora Prescription*. Connect with James online to receive the 7-day companion series, new book launch dates, and details on type-specific courses and live events—register at www.BurnItDown.online/begin or scan below.

References, Updates, and Amendments

At www.BurnItDown.online/references

Acknowledgments and Dedication

Emily Heckman, my editor—
thank you for always pushing me so hard.
Thanks to Jenna Sheridan for the jacket design.
And thanks to Alyssa, Carrie, Hanna,
and everyone at Dodd, Mead & Co.

For my parents—thank you for having me.

www.ingramcontent.com/pod-product-compliance
Lightning Source LLC
Chambersburg PA
CBHW021224130626
46554CB00004B/1355